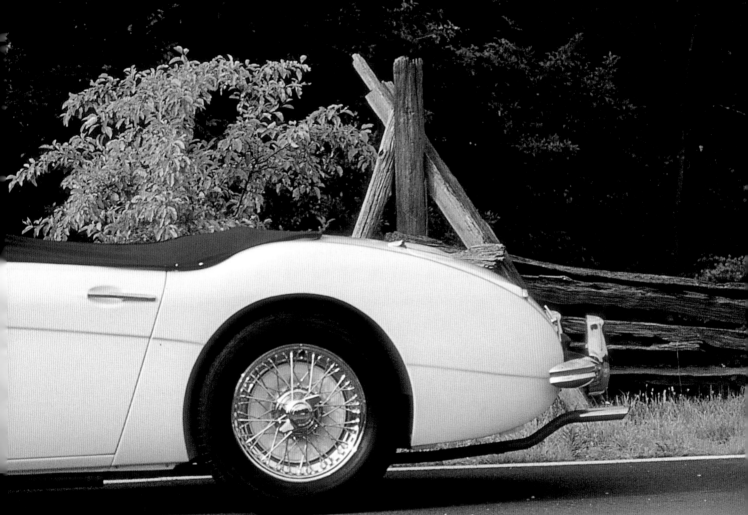

Austin-Healey
100 & 3000

John Heilig

MBI Publishing Company

To Florence, Susan, Sharon, and Laura,
whose love and support have kept me going
for all these years.

First published in 1995 by MBI Publishing Company,
PO Box 1, 729 Prospect Avenue, Osceola, WI 54020-0001 USA

© John Heilig, 1995

The information in this book is true and complete to the best of our knowledge. All recommendations are made without any guarantee on the part of the author or Publisher, who also disclaim any liability incurred in connection with the use of this data or specific details

We recognize that some words, model names, and designations, for example, mentioned herein are the property of the trademark holder. We use them for identification purposes only. This is not an official publication

MBI Publishing Company books are also available at discounts in bulk quantity for industrial or sales-promotional use. For details write to Special Sales Manager at Motorbooks International Wholesalers & Distributors, 729 Prospect Avenue, PO Box 1, Osceola, WI 54020-0001 USA

All photography by the author unless otherwise credited

Library of Congress Cataloging-in-Publication Data
Heilig, John.
    Austin-Healey 100 and 3000/John Heilig.
        p. cm.--(MBI Publishing Company sports car color history)
    Includes index.
    ISBN 0-7603-0060-7 (pbk.)
1. Austin-Healey automobile--History. I. Title. II. Series: Sports car color history.
TL215.A9H37   1995
629.222'27--dc20   95-13978

On the front cover: The ultimate Austin-Healey? Most enthusiasts would characterize the 100S as such, and with good reasons: a stellar racing history and production totaling only fifty. *David Gooley*

On the frontispiece: Simple and elegant lines keep the "big" Healey's body looking handsome in any era.

On the title page: The 100-6 clearly foreshadowed—in both body style and powerplant—the 3000 series cars that would follow.

On the back cover: Top: In British Racing Green, this early 100 easily looks the part of "quintessential British sports car." *David Gooley* Bottom: An early 3000 and an AC Ace-Bristol do battle in sunny California in March 1960. *Bob Tronolone*

Printed in Hong Kong

Contents

Acknowledgments

My first exposure to sports cars was in the late 1950s when I bought my first MGA. A co-worker sold it to me because he was moving up to an Austin-Healey. He needed the Healey for a variety of reasons, not the least of which was that the MG was too small for his 250-plus pound frame.

Over the course of the next five years, my girlfriend, fiancee, and wife (all the same person) and I made many new friends through sports cars. While these cars were primarily MGs and the friendships grew through the MG Car Club, there were the occasional Healeys in the crowd. One Healey owner was in our wedding party and we remained friends for many years.

But in time all things must change. We're not like Ray Carbone, who bought his Austin-Healey 3000 Mark II in 1963, drove it for a few years, then parked it in his garage for twenty more. When the urge moved him again, he dusted the Healey off, restored it, and has experienced a rebirth of sorts by driving the pristine white car all over the country. In our situation, we traded the MGA in on a 1965 Mustang fastback, then swapped again for a four-door sedan when daughters began arriving with alarming regularity. The next two steps took us into a station wagon and a full-sized van for transporting us and the three girls on vacations, to Girl Scouts, and then college.

The people I met, and you will meet in these pages, while working on this book are all Austin-Healey lovers. Most are beyond child-rearing age, although one or two bring the children along to Austin-Healey club meets. All these people accept the Healey's frailties with grace and aplomb. They know their cars can break (and do break) with alarming regularity, but they still love their machines.

When Motorbooks International asked me to write a book on the Big Healeys in the United States, I jumped at the chance. While I had never owned a Big Healey, they were always on the fringes of my sports car life, and I always coveted one. Through my conversations with Healey enthusiasts, I feel as if I have become a part of the Healey crowd.

The first person I spoke with was Geoffrey Healey–Donald Healey's son–who granted me a marvelous telephone interview in March 1994. Sadly, Geoff died April 29, 1994, and we were not able to develop our new friendship any further.

But I was fortunate in being able to discuss Austin-Healey development with many others in the small team that created these cars. To Barry Bilbie, Gerry Coker, and Roger Menadue I extend my sincere gratitude for sharing their memories.

In addition, I would like to thank Carroll Shelby, Steve Rossi, and Louise King for their memories of Donald Healey; Pat Moss-Carlsson, Stirling Moss, Dr. Dick Thompson, and Vincent Sardi for their experiences driving in competition for Donald Healey; and Mike Blatt, Ray Carbone, Jim Cox, Bob Eshelman, Jack Gerstein, Don Nally and Susan, Vincent Sardi, Ed Siegrist, Jerry Smith, Bob Tebbenhoff, Dave Venezia, and all the other Austin-Healey owners who so graciously shared their love for their cars and photographs from their collections.

A special thanks must go to photographers Dave Gooley and Mike Mueller, without whose assistance these cars would have been photographed with my Instamatic. In addition, Karla Rosenbush was of invaluable assistance with her fastidious editing.

Last, and definitely not least, my deep thanks to Motorbooks International Editor Zack Miller, who is responsible for the book's final form.

Handsome, purposeful, and fast, the 100S is the most desirable of the "big" Healeys.

Chapter 1

In the Beginning

Hollywood could have done it as a musical. Here was a group of Englishmen shortly after World War II–the Big One. They were just out of the armed services, and they were also out of work. Their country's manufacturing facilities were shattered during the war, and manufacturing materials in the postwar period were in short supply. The only way they could create employment for themselves was to develop a product that they could export, otherwise the materials of manufacture would be unavailable to them.

So, in the classic tradition of the Hollywood musical, they said, "let's build a car."

It's not that the idea was totally insane. There was, at the time, very little governmental regulation of the automotive industry. Their designs didn't have to be crash-tested to some government standard. And the group did know a little about building motor cars.

Heading the team was Donald Healey, who brought to the table a successful prewar rallying and racing career as well as experience designing cars for the late Triumph Motor Company (the Triumph name was owned by Standard in the postwar period). Healey had also worked for Humber during the war, primarily on military projects.

His chief associate was Achille C. "Sammy" Sampietro, who had experience designing cars with Humber before and during the war. Sampietro also

The Healey Silverstone is recognizable by its vertical "Healey" grille, cycle fenders, and headlights inset in the grille. Dave Gooley photo

operated a small consulting firm that was soon to run out of money and contribute another important player to the mix. Assisting Donald Healey was his son, Geoffrey, who was working for Armstrong-Siddley and had trained as an engineer before the war. Roger Menadue was another member of the small team. He had known Healey since 1926 when the two had met at Healey's garage in Perranporth. "He lived about six miles from where I lived," Menadue remembered. "I was apprenticed at a garage about six miles up the coast at Newquay."

Working nights and weekends in an attic above Healey's house in Cornwall, Healey and his associates designed a small, aerodynamic, Riley-powered sporting sedan and roadster that was to lead eventually to the creation of, first, the Healey Hundred (whose name was almost immediately changed to the *Austin*-Healey 100) and, later, the Austin-Healey 3000.

Of course, Healey's entry into the world of car manufacturing didn't "just happen." It came

about only after a long and successful competition career which included winning the 1931 Monte Carlo Rally at the wheel of an Invicta 4-1/2 liter.

Donald Mitchell Healey was born in Perranporth, Cornwall, in the west of England, on July 3, 1898. His father, John Frederick Healey, often referred to as J.F., was the town grocer, a business that became his when he left his job as a printing representative and married the store owner's daughter, Emmie Mitchell. Sometime later, he owned one of the first cars in the area, a 1908 Panhard et Levassor, a fact that wasn't lost on young Donald.

"Fortunately for me, Father was a speed enthusiast, insofar as he could be in those days," Donald remembered in his autobiography, *My World of Cars*, coauthored with Peter Garnier. "[The Panhard] was something pretty special where previously the only form of transport [in the area] had been horse-drawn carriages. It had a large four-cylinder engine, cast in two blocks of two cylinders each, and a hot-tube ignition. This was

Donald Healey seated in a Triumph Dolomite at Perranporth in 1934. This straight-eight supercharged car was a copy of the Alfa Romeo 2300, but the copying was done with the full cooperation of Vittorio Jano of Alfa, *whose feeling was that it was a dated design anyway and imitation was a form of flattery.* Roger Menadue photo

Workers at Warwick assembling a Healey Elliot sedan. The Elliot was so named because bodies were built by Elliots of Reading. Westland Aeroparts built the Healey

Westlands roadster version of the same chassis/engine combination.

later converted to a chain-driven Bosch magneto, which transformed the running, but was responsible for breaking [my father's] arm on one occasion when it backfired while he was cranking it."

Donald admitted to being "keenly interested" in cars and airplanes as a youth. He attended Newquay College, where he majored in physics. He decided that his future was in airplanes and

wrote to Sopwith, creator of the famed Sopwith Camel, asking to be admitted as a pupil. He was accepted, provided his father would agree, which he did. J.F. also supplied the tuition payment of £250. The engineering training Donald received at Sopwith would help him discover a career once he was mustered out of the service at World War I's end.

Donald Healey at the wheel of Healey Number 1, a Westland-bodied roadster. This car was the result of teamwork among some World War II buddies—Healey, son Geoff Healey, Roger Menadue, and Barry Bilbie.

The car used a 2.4-liter Riley engine and a body built by Westland Aeroparts, hence the name. The body was designed by Ben Bowden. Roger Menadue photo

The first world war threw a monkey wrench into many young men's plans. Donald lied about his age in order to join the infantry, which he thought would ease his entry into the Royal Flying Corps. J.F., however, revealed the truth and had the enlistment canceled, returning Donald to Sopwith. When he turned eighteen, Donald joined the RFC legally and eventually learned how to fly. His flying career came to an abrupt halt when he crashed into a grandstand at Doncaster race course on July 30, 1916, with little injury to himself but significant injury to the airplane.

When Donald returned to Perranporth, he talked J.F. into backing his opening of a small auto repair garage. "Often a day would pass without one's ever *seeing* a car," he wrote. "It was in this atmosphere of doubt and misgiving [about the future of the automobile] that I had to sell my father my absolute conviction that there would be the need for a garage in Perranporth. I shall not forget my gratitude when he agreed to the idea."

Ever the entrepreneur, Healey also bought a 1921 six-cylinder Buick (with the assistance of his father again) and used it and a small BSA for a taxi service. Healey's drivers would pick up people at the rail stations in Truro and Chacewater and deliver them to the resorts in Perranporth and Newquay, the "Cornish Riviera." Next he invested in a charbanc coach and had a twenty-five-seat body fitted to expand into bus service. The car service fleet would eventually grow to include his father's 1908 American RMC underslung tourer, a 30 hp Armstrong-Siddley, and two 1914 Rolls-Royces. Here was a man on the go.

About this time Healey also discovered competition—specifically rallys and trials. The garage and taxi business didn't suffer because he had good people working for him, but he began spending less and less time in Perranporth.

The Buick was his first competition car when he entered a speed trial run by the Truro Motor Club in 1921. Stripping the Buick of its mudguards and windshield, he was able to push it to 66 mph on a straight stretch of road near Perranporth.

In 1922, Healey bought an ABC and an Ariel 10 to use as a trials car, and an early Riley Redwinger for rallying. The Ariel was credited with 52.2 mpg in the 1922 Land's End Trial, which aided Healey on another front because his garage was the Ariel agency in Cornwall. After bringing the charred Riley chassis home, he picked up his ABC, called the organizers about the change in entry, and promptly won a gold medal in the 1924 Land's End Trial.

A friendship with Gordon Parnell, chief engineer of the Triumph Company (for which Healey also had a dealership), earned him rides in "the most unlikely-looking Triumph Seven and Super Seven family saloons in all sorts of events." Healey's first major success was in 1928 when he won the Bournemouth Rally—predecessor of today's RAC Rally—in an 832 cc Triumph Super Seven.

In 1929, he entered the Super Seven in the Monte Carlo Rally, even though he had never even driven on the continent. He and Tommy Wisdom won the Mont-des-Mules Trophy for best time on that hillclimb. The next year they finished seventh overall and were the top-placed British team.

With his competition career now in full bloom, the little garage in Perranporth must have held less of a challenge for Healey. He joined the Invicta team in 1930, which in those days meant being provided with cars by Noel Macklin, Invicta's creator. In his autobiography, Healey relates how he was chosen for the team:

> When Noel Macklin began to seek publicity for his cars in international rallies in 1930, he approached Humphrey Symonds of *The Motor* . . . for suggestions as to who should drive for him. Humphrey searched his mind: "I know," he said, "there's a chap called Donald Healey—lives down in Cornwall. He's done pretty well in long-distance events recently. Why don't you have a word with him?"

Macklin and Healey "had a word," and Donald began driving Invictas in competition. The first car was the 4-1/2-ltr model, which Healey used to become European hill climb champion. For 1931, Macklin had developed a better version of the 4-1/2 ltr, called the S-Type, which featured a very light and flexible Weymann body and a truck gearbox. Healey, Humphrey Symonds, and Lewis Pearce co-drove the S-Type in the 1931 Monte

Donald Healey (left) and Roger Menadue on the Jabbeke Autostrada in 1947 just after they had captured several world records for production cars. With a speed of more than 110 mph over a measured mile, the Healey was proclaimed the fastest British production car. Roger Menadue photo

Carlo Rally and, despite a minor accident which required sawing off one of the brake rods and finishing the event with three-wheel braking, they won.

"My greatest ambition had been to win the Monte," he wrote, "and I can't describe my joy. I telephoned my wife (Ivy) to come out for the celebration. Having no passport, she approached the home secretary direct, who had a special passport issued because of the British success, and she came out to join in the fun and visit the Palace for the prize presentation by Prince Ranier."

(Incidentally, the association with Noel Macklin was returned when Noel's son, Lance, became one of the prime drivers of Austin-Healey race cars.)

Healey finished second in the 1932 Monte in an Invicta but crashed in 1933.

"In the early 1930s Donald went up to Coventry, which was the center of the motor industry in Great Britain in those days," Roger Menadue remembered. "I joined him up there in 1936." Menadue continued:

> He went first of all to Riley, who invited him up. After about two or three months, Triumph, who he also used to drive for in rallies, offered him the job of chief engineer to the company which was a better job. So he took that. But there was no animosity or anything with Riley. Of course they just realized that was what anybody would do.
>
> It was a completely different business in those days. It was always a friendly sort of show and

everyone helped one another. Today it's so different. You couldn't recognize it as the same industry.

The people who built the companies in those days were the engineers, you see. And then the money people took over, and it's become a different thing. It's a money affair today.

In 1934, Healey became Experimental Manager at Triumph after he told Colonel Holbrook, then Managing Director, that if the Triumph 10 Gloria "was going to compete with the Riley they'd have to get someone on their payroll with sufficient experience to put it right." That someone, of course, became Donald Healey.

Healey worked on the Gloria and modified it in preparation for the 1934 Monte Carlo Rally. His co-drivers were Norman Bleach and Tommy Wisdom (who would later lend his daughter Ann to future Austin-Healey successes). They finished third, earning Healey the Coupe de l'Illustration Automobile Trophy for having finished in each of the top three places.

Triumph was seeking to develop a sports car that would be somewhat better than the tiny MG Midget and Singer Le Mans. The company also wanted to have a model to compete with what were considered the ultimate sports cars of the time–the 2.3 ltr and 1750 cc Alfa Romeos. One day Tommy Wisdom joined Healey for lunch at the Triumph factory and a legend was born.

With a little encouragement from Wisdom, it's not surprising that Healey chose to imitate a more successful car in the design of what would become his first car. In this case, the car they imitated was the 2.3 ltr Alfa, and the result was the Triumph Dolomite. Healey wrote:

The Westland roadster in which Healey is seated had a successful competition life and was the first Healey-badged car to be brought to the United States.

The Westland roadster in a showroom, ready for sale.

It was . . . Tom's idea to get hold of an Alfa Romeo, strip down the engine to the very last nut and bolt, and inspect it, in an effort to establish what made it such an outstandingly successful design. So far as I personally was concerned, I was not averse to the unreasonably frowned-upon practice of copying–or let's say seeking inspiration from–someone else's design. I consider this to be the whole essence of being a successful motor-car designer–the ability to select the best features from the individual designs of each of one's main rivals, and embody them in a winning whole. Greater manufacturers than Triumph have done this unashamedly and without being pilloried both before and since.

The background to the exciting and stylish straight-eight, supercharged Triumph Dolomite that resulted has always been wrapped in mystery, so far as the public was concerned, with unfounded tales of lawsuits, plagiarism, and suchlike through the years. There was, in fact, nothing mysterious about it, the whole operation being carried out with complete co-operation from Alfa Romeo.

Roger Menadue seated in one of the first Silverstones just before it is was loaded on the Queen Elizabeth for its trip to New York and the New York Auto Show. Silverstones proved to be popular racers in Europe and the United States. Briggs Cunningham is one of the drivers who replaced the Riley engine with a larger American design. Roger Menadue photo

The Silverstone used the 2.4-liter Riley engine, as did all pre-Austin-Healey Healeys. Dave Gooley photo

Healey used a ladder-type chassis frame with a 104-inch wheelbase, beam axles, and semi-elliptic springs front and rear. In this case, Alfa's design didn't work. The engine was a supercharged 2.3-ltr straight eight. Alfa engineer Vittorio Jano, who had designed the engine, was thrilled that as prestigious a British manufacturer such as Triumph would be interested in copying his engine. Since it was beginning to show its age anyway, Jano aided Triumph, and there was no hint of plagiarism.

The Dolomite was a manufacturing and artistic success. However, its competition debut was less than stellar. Donald and Lewis Pearce entered the prototype car in the 1935 Monte Carlo Rally which started in Sweden. During the first night, Healey was following another car with his lights out in order to conserve the batteries when he heard a loud screech. He thought at first that the supercharger was seizing. Immediately after, there was a loud crash, and the car spun around in a complete circle. They had been hit by a train. Fortunately, the only human damage was the loss of a tooth by Pearce. Healey came back with the Dolomite in 1936 to finish eighth in the Monte. He

retired in the 1937 event with engine trouble in his Triumph 12.

Triumph built the Dolomite and variations of it until 1939. Healey was responsible for the design of all Triumph cars from 1934 to 1938. Unfortunately, the company was not doing well financially, and it went into receivership in 1939. Healey tried to buy the company but was unsuccessful. Eventually, the Air Ministry bought the factories–there was a new war beginning to stir–and Standard bought the Triumph name.

With the closing of Triumph, Healey was out of a job, but not for long. The specter of war loomed over Europe, and someone with Healey's engineering expertise could not go unused for long. The Air Ministry asked him to stay on at the factory, building Claudel-Hobson carburetors for airplane engines. Healey accepted with glee when he discovered that Vauxhall designer Laurence Pomeroy Sr. was going to be the factory's director. In addition, Healey accepted a commission from the RAFVR as a liaison officer arranging flying programs.

After the War

There aren't a lot of positive things that can be said for World War II. Just about the only outcome of any merit (other than the Allied victory, of course) is that the war forged some strong alliances–between nations, between companies, and between men.

For Donald Healey, World War II introduced him to some new, creative minds and reinforced friendships made before the war. These friendships would lead Healey in a new direction. While it wasn't that far removed from the direction he was following at Triumph–designing ever better automobiles–this time he was to strike out on his own and build automobiles that would carry his name.

Healey stayed at the former Triumph factory until Laurence Pomeroy died, then Healey left this post and joined the Humber Car Company to design military vehicles. He felt this would make better use of his automotive design knowledge.

At Humber, Healey met Ben Bowden and Sammy Sampietro. Bowden was Humber's chief body draftsman, and Sampietro was a chassis designer. The three of them began discussing what they would do when the war ended and decided that what they wanted to do was design and build automobiles.

Meanwhile, Geoffrey Healey was beginning to make his mark. Born on December 14, 1922, Geoff studied engineering at the Camborne School

A Healey Silverstone on the Alpine Rally. The first competition event for the car was the Alpine of 1949 where Donald Healey and Ian Appleyard finished second overall and won their class.

Mines. He joined Cornercroft in Coventry as an apprentice while studying for his exams in order to earn his Higher National Certificate in Engineering at the Coventry Technical College. In 1943, he joined the Royal Electrical and Mechanical Engineers (equivalent to the U.S. Army Corps of Engineers). He was commissioned as a second lieutenant in 1944 and was later promoted to first lieutenant. In 1945, he was promoted to captain and served in Lebanon.

After the war ended, and while Donald Healey, Bowden, and Sampietro still worked at Humber, they spent evenings and weekends working together on the design of a new sports car. Geoff would come home on leaves and assist. He continued to work with the small crew headed by his father even after he left the service and joined Armstrong-Siddley in 1947. Donald Healey and company's goal was to build a British car that could compete with the prewar BMW 328, which was considered the best sports car of its time.

"We had always talked about building our own car when we were at Triumph," Roger Menadue remembered:

But Triumph was rather frustrating because they hadn't a lot of money, and they weren't interested in going into a lot of the radical sports things that we wanted to go into. We were building the car before the end of the war and finished it in 1945. The war was going well without us. We had invaded the continent and we could see that things

Nash supplied the 3.8- and 4.1-liter inline six engine for the Nash-Healey. Without the assistance of Nash-Kelvinator, it is likely Healey Motors would have gone out of business. Dave Gooley photo

Previous page
The Pininfarina-designed Nash-Healey coupe was an attractive car in its era (1950). Of 506 Nash-Healeys that were built, 151 had Pininfarina-designed bodies. It still retained the Nash grille, which Donald didn't like, and the 4.1-liter six-cylinder engine, which he did like. Dave Gooley photo

were going to be tied up in a reasonable time. Of course we were working for the government. I worked with Armstrong-Whitworth, Donald was with Humber, and Gerry Coker was also with Humber; that's where he met Donald.

Donald Healey had developed a friendship with Victor Riley of Riley Motors, which had just been bought by Lord Nuffield of Morris Motors. Riley had developed a 2.4-ltr four-cylinder engine that produced slightly more than 100 hp—just about the power level the conspirators wanted for their new car. Victor Riley supplied Healey with one of the new engines, a gearbox, and rear axle for the prototype.

By this time (1946) Donald Healey had left Humber to established himself in business. "My chief problem [was to] find somewhere to build the prototype chassis," he wrote. "An old friend and Triumph co-director, Wally Allen, owned a works in Warwick making cement mixers, and he personally offered me the use of one of his sheds.

Permits for steel had to be obtained from the Ministry of Supply; we had no background of prewar production, and it was extremely difficult to convince them that we really intended to build cars with an export potential, this being their principal condition for allocating us the materials we required."

Through Riley's supply manager, Jack Tatton, Healey was able to obtain a permit to purchase a limited amount of steel to build cars.

Westland Aeroparts built the prototype chassis. The side rails were 7 ft, 6 in long because the largest metal folding machine available would accommodate a maximum length of eight feet. Sampietro designed a trailing link independent front suspension, which was expensive for the era but was considered to be the best system available.

The chassis was eventually completed, but the car still lacked a name. Healey wrote, "My first thought was 'Invicta,' as they were then out of business, but Earl Fitzwilliam, who owned the name, would not part with it. I tried to recall all the noteworthy wartime names, even Winston Churchill, and practically settled upon 'Crusader.' I went to my old friend Victor Riley for his advice. He looked at all my suggestions and then said, 'What's wrong with your own name?—it sounds right, and you already have a good record as a sports car designer.' So the car became the Healey 2.4 ltr."

The use of the Healey name on the car proved to be a good omen. *Autocar*'s review of January 4, 1946, noted:

> Donald Healey, the well-known and highly successful driver in international trials, rallies, and other competitions, has designed and is about to put on the market a car of his own. It will attract the immediate attention of enthusiasts the world over because its construction meets so many points which could only be understood by people who have handled fast cars in the major sporting events.
>
> Personal experience has shown Donald Healey that a fast car is not really a fast car unless it holds the road. Holding the road means that the car is completely stable and will invariably obey the control of the driver at all speeds of which it is capable, and under all road conditions.

Of course, this last trait that would mark every car to bear the Healey name.

Ben Bowden designed two bodies: a sedan and a convertible. Each was built by a different body building company which loaned its name to the car. The "Healey Elliot Saloon" was built by Elliots of Reading while the "Healey Westland Roadster" was built by Westland Aeroparts of Hereford, which had also built the prototype chassis frame. The Westland was given chassis number 1501 and registration number VVV214. According to Donald, the chassis number meant absolutely nothing and the registration number was false as well, being concocted from a supply of the letter "V" and some spare numbers.

Between 1946 and 1954, Healey and his small company built six different models based on Riley components. All used the Riley twin-cam 2.4-ltr four-cylinder engine and gearbox, which Victor Riley had agreed to supply to Healey. These engines were rated at 104 bhp at 4,500 rpm and used twin 1-1/2 in SU carburetors. But despite the variety of products based on similar components, only 1,114 cars were built. The development and production of these cars, however, did give the Donald Healey Motor Company the experience necessary to grow.

The first major test of the Riley-engined sedan was in the spring of 1946 when Christopher Jennings, the editor of *Motor*, took the car to Italy. Jennings was able to wring 106.56 mph out of the sedan on the Como-Milan Autostrada. His report enthused, "no other car has been timed by the *Motor* at so high a speed."

In March 1947, Donald and Geoff took the roadster on a trip to the United States to test the waters for possible sales. Besides learning that there was indeed a market for well-built cars that handled well, Geoff caught a disease–the Hot Rod Bug. He wrote, "I came home full of enthusiasm for the idea, determined to build a car of that type." Eventually he built a car using a Canadian-built Ford V-8 tank engine and some scrap Healey parts, including the discarded prototype frame. Geoff drove this car to fastest time of the day in a Nottingham Sports Car Club meeting and eventually formed the British Hot Rod Association with a group of friends.

In 1948, Geoff was given time off from Armstrong-Siddley to accompany his father on their first Mille Miglia in a Westland-bodied roadster. Johnny Lurani drove a sedan. Despite some mechanical problems, not the least of which was an electrical problem that cropped up when the Healeys hit a small dog, they finished ninth overall and fourth in the unlimited sports car class. Lurani finished thirteenth and won the touring category.

Donald entered a Healey in the 1949 Monte Carlo Rally but had to retire when the third-gear

One of the minor styling drawbacks of the Nash-Healey was the required use of the large Nash grille. Dave Gooley photo

synchro hub broke on the Riley gearbox, a common problem.

The first Healeys used what has been referred to as the "A-Type" chassis. This was used for about six months until it was replaced by the "B-Type," which had an adjustable steering column, single 12-volt battery (instead of two 6-volt units), and fuel pumps located in the trunk. In 1950, the "C–Type" chassis was introduced; it featured a modified front suspension.

A different version of the roadster was built by Duncan bodies on the B-Type chassis in 1950. It was less expensive and roomier than the original Elliot- and Westland-bodied cars. The final car constructed on the B chassis was the Sportsmobile, a luxurious four-seater that was built from 1948 to 1950.

Healey Silverstone

With the D-Type chassis in 1949 came the Silverstone, an open two-seat sports-cum-race car with a lightweight aluminum body. The Silverstone was a pure competition car with only lip service paid to creature comforts. While it still used the same Riley engine rated at 104 bhp, it had removable cycle fenders, a windshield that could be lowered, and headlights mounted close together behind the grille (additional lights could be added for night-time events). Donald and Ian Appleyard entered a Silverstone in the 1949 Alpine Rally and finished second, an impressive competition debut for the car.

In the Silverstone, the engine was moved back eight inches compared to the earlier cars, the suspension was beefed up with an antiroll bar and stiffer springs, and *narrower* tires (5.50x15 versus the standard 5.75x15) were added. The spare was installed in a slot at the rear of the car and served as a bumper.

Cameron Argetsinger, who was responsible for the creation of the Watkins Glen race course, fondly remembers the Healey Silverstone he bought for the 1949 Watkins Glen Grand Prix:

I liked that car. I liked it a lot. When I first got it, I drove it from New York City back to Watkins Glen and then to Youngstown, Ohio. I took the shortcut from Watkins Glen across the mountains of Pennsylvania. The fenders fell off. My son Jason was about seven or eight at the time. He

The Nash-Healey Pininfarina roadster was a classic 1950s sports car. While it didn't have bucket seats, it did have a bench wide enough for three passengers, a decent trunk, and good power to provide decent performance. It also had a Healey-designed suspension.

Bench seats and a spartan dash are not what one would normally expect in a sports car, but they were part of the Nash-Healey.

was on the passenger seat on the left, and he was holding one fender on. I was in the driver's seat on the right, driving with one hand and holding the other one on.

We took the car to Cornell Labs, and they fixed that, but they broke a push rod. It wasn't over-revved. It had the 2.4-ltr engine. I had ordered high-compression pistons from Max Hoffman, but they weren't ready. So I got some Jahn's pistons, and they were installed at Cornell Lab. The car really ran very well.

I was charging up the back hill with my crew chief on the Monday before the race, and I had an ignition problem. I blew a hole in the piston. So I coasted up the hill and around the bend to my grandmother's house. Meanwhile, during the summer, Max Hoffman delivered the high compression pistons that were supposed to be delivered with the car. When they installed the high compression pistons the lug nuts kept breaking. They wouldn't stick every time they torqued it down. So we solved that with Buick lug nuts. But the engine

blew going up the hill when I bent a push rod. [A local garage] just straightened it. It broke during the race. I later replaced it with a Buick push rod that gave me no problems.

Nash-Healey

Late in 1949, Donald was once again on his way across the Atlantic to gauge the American market and to see about obtaining engines for his cars. Briggs Cunningham had improved the performance of his Silverstone by replacing the stock powerplant with a 5.5-ltr Cadillac engine and had raced it successfully at the first Watkins Glen race in October 1948. Donald wanted to see if there was any possibility of obtaining a supply of Caddy engines.

"My father was going to see Ed Cole at General Motors at the time," Geoff Healey remembered.

He had been to the United States several times and was sailing on the *Queen Elizabeth*.

From the rear, the Nash-Healey shows design trends that would emerge later in the Austin-Healey.

While he was on the boat he met George Mason, who was president of Nash-Kelvinator. My father and he talked on the boat, having the common interests of automobiles and cameras. George Mason said, "When you're through seeing Ed Cole come along and see me. I might be able to suggest something that will interest you. We've got a good engine, and we'd like to talk."

Donald wrote in his book that Mason told him: "See if you can get engines [from Cole]—and if you fail, come back and have a chat with me. I'd like very much to make a smaller car than the usual run of American cars, and I'd like it to be a sports car—about the size of your Silverstone. We can introduce you to my right-hand man, George Romney, and we'll chat about the possibilities of getting together."

As it turned out, General Motors wasn't interested in supplying engines to a small, British car builder, but George Mason and Nash were. The result was the Nash-Healey.

Geoff was working for Armstrong-Siddley in 1948. When he left that firm at the end of 1949 to join his father, work was just beginning on the Nash-Healey. With Roger Menadue, Geoff developed the competition version of the car.

At the same time, an old friend of Sammy Sampietro was becoming dissatisfied with the company he was working with and was looking for a change. Gerry Coker remembers:

I had worked with Sampietro in London as a consultant, as his designer. I'd also served a lot of my apprenticeship under him at Rootes. He approached me one time and said he needed a designer in this consulting company he and his partners were starting to do electromagnetic coupling. I went to work for him for two years, and then the money ran out.

Then I went to Armstrong-Whitworth aircraft as a designer on turbines. Well, I didn't design the turbine blades. It was most boring. Eventually I talked to Sammy, and he asked, "How are you getting on?" I said, "I can't stand it!" He said a friend of his–Don Healey–was looking for an engineer and told me he thought I'd do fine. He set up an appointment and I went to talk with Don.

I met Don Healey at his house, showed him what I could do, and that's when I started. He needed an engineer to follow up on the Nash-Healey cars that he was producing. They were building the chassis at Warwick, and they were having the aluminum bodies built by a firm in Birmingham. I came in to oversee the production of these bodies and make sure they did this, that, and the other.

The Nash-Healey did more than provide Donald Healey with a 3.8-ltr (later 4.1) engine and entry into the American market. It also saved his company. Healey owed the bank something like £50,000. His father had extended himself in order to back Donald, and Healey's father's financial situation was not strong. "I explained all this to

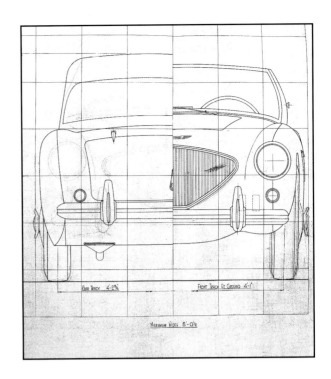

Gerry Coker's original plans for the Healey Hundred (later Austin-Healey 100). Front and rear views show that it was, indeed, designed as a left-hand-drive car.

A design from Coker's drawing board showing how the Healey might have looked as a coupe.

An interesting, Coker-penned variation on the Austin-Healey design.

George Romney," Donald wrote. "And he said: 'Well, don't let that worry you. Let's get together over the practical side of production, shipping, marketing, and so on while you're getting on with building the prototype, which we'll pay for.'" Ultimately, Healey was able to provide an introduction for Mason to the Austin Motor Company, a partnership that resulted in the Nash Metropolitan.

Eventually Nash-Kelvinator paid off Healey's bank loans, which Healey paid back in finished cars. "Without them, I could not have carried on," Healey wrote. "I simply could not afford to build the prototype, or to employ the men to do the work, or even keep our little place going on the small profits made by such cars as the Silverstone."

While the Nash-Healey was still in the development stage, Gerry Coker took one of the styling drawings and was looking at it in his office when Healey came in. "Don asked me what I had," Coker remembered.

I said, "It's your Nash-Healey. This line isn't really right on the rear fender." I thought to myself it was bloody cheeky really, me telling him what his styling is. But I told him I thought it would be more natural for the lower edge of the fender to be about four inches lower. So I drew it on there and he said, "Oh, yes. I didn't know that. Can you have it changed?"

Coker made the change, along with a few others he suggested and Healey approved. That's how he became involved in car styling. He had been hired as an engineer, but Healey soon discovered that he had a stylist on the staff as well as someone who understood spot-welding.

Healey liked the Nash-Healey and the power it offered. One of the conditions of the engine supply, however, was contingent upon use of the wide Nash grille, which gave the car what Healey called a "Joe E. Brown" front.

Geoff was able to make the car handle fairly well, even with the heavy, front-mounted engine. They entered the prototype in the 1950 Mille Miglia, driven by Donald and Geoff. They finished ninth in class and 177th out of 383 entrants. In June, with Tony Rolt and Duncan Hamilton sharing the driving, the car finished fourth overall at Le Mans. The following year Donald and Geoff were thirtieth in the Mille Miglia, with Rolt and Hamilton sixth overall at Le Mans. They were third overall in 1952.

Riley-engined car production ceased in the summer of 1950 with the shift to full production of the Nash-Healey. By August 1954, when the last Nash-Healey was shipped to the United States, 506 Nash-Healeys had been built, including 151 with special Pininfarina bodies. But by then, there was another car in the winds.

First, Healey tried installing an Alvis engine in a Nash-Healey chassis. That wasn't successful. Although the performance was adequate, only twenty-five were built. Next, through a connection with Leonard Lord, who headed the Austin Motor Company, Healey tried installing the 2.6-ltr four-cylinder Austin engine in a new chassis. This was a successful marriage, and the new engine/chassis combination would provide Donald Healey entrée to the world of major automobile manufacturers.

*The original Healey Hundred before its trip to the Earls
Court Motor Show.* Gerry Coker photo

Chapter 2

The Austin-Healey 100

Parliament realized that one way to feed necessary money into the struggling British financial system was to sell products to the United States forces stationed in Europe and export them to the U.S. as well. Auto manufacturers were especially encouraged to export to the States. Those with viable export plans would be allotted the raw materials to produce these items for export. What England needed was cash.

And the Nash-Healey wasn't helping that much. "We couldn't sell the Nash in Great Britain because of the dollar problem," Roger Menadue remembered.

It had the American engine and the government wouldn't allow us to sell American things in this country because of the cost of dollars. At the end of the war, you see, we were bankrupt. We had no dollars or any darned thing. If it wasn't for Lend Lease, with the Americans lending us all this equipment and that sort of thing, we should have been sunk. We didn't have any money to buy on the world market. We'd spent all our dollars because war is a very costly business and we ran out of dollars. So we had to get in as many dollars as possible.

With the windshield folded, the Austin-Healey 100 is as sleek as any road car. Gerry Coker designed a simple folding mechanism for the windshield that made it more aerodynamic for competition.

Production line at The Cape, Warwick. Healey built the first 100 pre-production cars and remained as the producer of all competition Austin-Healeys through the life of the cars. Formal production took place at Longbridge and later Abingdon. Healey engineers frequently had difficulties working with unionized crews at these two plants rather than the loose-knit crew at Warwick.

Donald Healey knew this as well as anyone from his frequent visits across the Atlantic. He knew the potential in the American market. But sales of the Nash-Healey were in the doldrums, and the car never sold as well as the Healeys thought it would, according to chassis designer Barry Bilbie. But Healey had developed an excellent reputation for the quality of his cars as well as his competition successes. Healey took the knowledge of what he thought the Americans wanted and began work on a new car. He thought the MG was too small and the Jaguar was too expensive. What he wanted was a car that would fit somewhere between those two in size and price. The result of that desire was the Healey Hundred.

Geoff Healey was the chief engineer on the Healey Hundred, in charge of all design and development. "The Hundred started from a clean sheet of paper," Geoff remembered. "There was virtually no carryover from any of the earlier cars. What we aimed to do was produce a low-cost sports car. The [use of] Austin components was one way of doing it. Not only that, they proved to be extremely reliable. It was the first time we had used Austin components in a car. Previously we had used Riley and Alvis components."

Donald Healey's aim was to make a car that could exceed 100 mph, thus, the name. Many cars of this period were named after their engine size or

top speed. The Jaguar XK120, XK140, and XK150 were, allegedly, named after their top speeds, while the Jaguar 3.4 sedan was powered by a 3.4-ltr engine. "Most cars they called '90' never did 90 mph, though," Geoffrey Healey said.

Donald, Geoffrey, and the others in the Healey Hundred development team, therefore, drew up a list of all the cars that could exceed 100 mph and used them as benchmarks. There weren't that many at the time. Of course, the Jaguar could do 100, but it was out of the price range the Healeys were aiming for. Most of the cars capable of such a speed simply cost too much. And the cars that were economical, like the MG, were too small to attain the speed, although they delivered stirring performance and gave exciting rides.

By 1951, Donald and Geoff began talking about a car that would meet the speed expectation and be economical as well. "All the original design work took place at home in the evenings," Geoff wrote, "as we did not want any knowledge of the fact that we were considering the use of Austin units to leak out to our normal supplier, Morris Motors. Morris and Austin had been great rivals in the motor world and it might jeopardize our supply of the 2.4-ltr Riley unit [from Morris]."

But the Healeys were certain that the future of the Riley units was dim (it was; while Riley continued production as an independent marque until 1963, Riley was, in fact, a minor player in the British industry). Healey knew the axles were due to go out of production and the expensive engine could follow shortly.

The press was enthusiastic about an Austin A90, which was powered by a 2,660 cc four-cylinder engine. The engine developed about 80 hp in A90 trim, but Donald knew output could be increased with induction manifold and carburetor modifications. Of prime importance, the engine was available in large quantities at a price below that of the Riley. Donald Healey later explained, "With my particular way of making motor cars, success is entirely dependent upon getting as many parts as is possible from a standard, production model. It is the tooling for these small bits and pieces that can bite into the profit margin of a limited-production car."

Donald approached Leonard Lord, head of Austin, with regard to Austin supplying engines for a new Healey model. Lord approved.

After Donald and Geoff had established a basic layout using the A90 engine, suspension, and drivetrain, Donald sketched a basic body form and took the sketches to Warwick, where they had been building bodies for the other Healey models. Barry Bilbie, a chassis designer, and Gerry Coker, a body designer, began preparing prototype drawings. Gerry Coker remembered:

Don came into the office one day and Geoff was there and Barry Bilbie, who was Geoff's chassis designer, was there, and I was there. He [Donald Healey] said there was this big opening between the MG and the Jag, and he told Geoff what he'd like to use for an engine and transmission and suspension. And he said to me "you do the body, Gerry, and let me see what you can come up with."

So I started on that, working with Geoff's engine height, wheelbase, and tread and so on.

There were three of us in the drawing office: a boy learning to be a draftsman, a chassis designer [Barry Bilbie], and me. I was very into Italian styling; I thought they had the greatest styling. So he [Donald] was going to get an Italian car. Healey didn't know what he wanted, but I knew what I liked.

Coker designed an aerodynamic two-seater with left-hand drive and small fins on the rear fenders. "Don hated the fins and before the next

The Healey Hundred on the stand at the 1952 London Motor Show. Donald Healey still wasn't happy with the grille design, so he had the car positioned such that the grille wouldn't show. Leonard Lord, head of BMC, liked the car, though, and offered to build it as the Austin-Healey. Gerry Coker photo

Healey Hundred with the trunk lid open showing the basic construction of the car. The car was built of 3-in square, box-section side-members with box-section cross-members used as bracing. The cross-members can be seen in the trunk. Gerry Coker photo

The Healey Hundred. Note that the grille has the pointed peak, which was softened for the Austin-Healey 100.

step they were removed," Coker said. "We did the car for the American market, and I had these tail fins on it."

On the other side I had it as pure as it finished up. Tickford got the job of doing the prototype. Don came in one day and said, "Let's go and see how they're getting on with the prototype." So we go in there, and they had these aluminum panels clamped over the wooden egg-crate jig. I had spent some time out there with the layout people making sure the lines were what I had drawn in Warwick. There was a chap named Bert Thigpenny, who was excellent. He was a surface layout draftsman. He'd take these lines from my drawing, and I'd just sit there and he'd say, "Is this what you want?" And I'd say, "Not really, Bert. I thought it would be a bit higher there or a bit smoother

Though the Healey Hundred was designed as a left-hand-drive car (as shown), it was also built as a right-hand-drive. Gerry Coker photo

there." And he'd say, "Like this?," and I'd say, "That's fine." That's how we did it.

When the panels were done and clamped on the wooden egg-crate, we went down there. One side was a fin, for America, and one side was the way it should be, for a pure sports car. We looked at it and Don said, "What do you think?" And I said, "Well, I don't really like it. I don't think it's really up, is it?" And he said, "No, it isn't. Let's not do it. Let's do the pure side, without the fins." That's how that went. You really can't tell what the car's going to look like until you see it in three dimensions.

The Healey Hundred was one of the few cars that looked good with two-tone paint, yet according to Coker it wasn't designed that way. Healey particularly didn't care for the treatment. Coker showed Healey the side view just before Donald

left on another of his trips to the United States. "See what you can do when I come back," was his charge to Coker about the side treatment.

"I tried for the two weeks that he was away and that was the best thing that I could come up with," Coker said.

So I made a full-sized drawing and cut it out and pinned it on my full-sized board, which was vertical so it was road height. When Don walked

Next page
With its top up, the Austin-Healey 100 still looks good. Gerry Coker designed the 100 as a left-hand drive car with the full intention that it would be exported to the United States. In fact, over 75 percent of all Austin-Healeys were exported. Chrome wire wheels are non-standard as are fender-mounted mirrors.

When Leonard Lord offered to build the Austin-Healey 100, Gerry Coker had to design a new badge for the car overnight.

into the office, the first thing he sees is the silhouette of this car, the same one that I'm trying to sell.

Don said, "Good morning, Gerry. You're still trying to sell that thing?" And I told him it was the best I could do. So he said, "Alright, make a clay model of it and see what it looks like." That's what he was like.

But Coker thought the side profile was too plain. It needed something to jazz it up, so he added a character line. "It didn't *do* anything, it didn't *mean* anything," he remembered. "But the car needed something to give it length and make it look lower. If I designed one today, I'd still have to put that line on somewhere."

Coker thought of adding an air exit hole at the leading edge of the style line to let hot air out of the engine. "I needed a motif or something to lead this line," he said. "I had a Parker fountain pen that had a very nice arrow on the clip. I tried that and it looked flaky. So then I tried it cut in half, and that's really how the spear came on there."

The original design also incorporated a triangular grille and bulges in the hood to clear the twin SU carburetors. The bulges were deleted early while the grille's shape was softened by flattening the top.

One of the more unique features of the Healey Hundred was its folding windshield. Coker designed a simple mechanism to fold the windshield

and secure it with thumb-screws in the lowered position. This reduced the frontal area for any owners who were interested in competing with their cars.

Chassis

Underneath Coker's body was a ladder-frame chassis comprised of two 3-in box rails. In order to keep performance high, the car's overall dimensions were kept small. Coker often told Geoff Healey that his (Coker's) job was to cover up the mess Geoff and his engineers made underneath.

Barry Bilbie, who had done his apprentice training at Maudslay Motor Co., working on trucks, had been promoted from junior draftsman to senior draftsman when the previous senior draftsman left Healey. Bilbie designed the underslung frame which created a tremendous aftermarket for mufflers and exhaust systems that were torn off when drivers ventured out on roads with high crowns. Bilbie had made the Nash-Healey and its outdated trailing link suspension work, so Donald Healey had confidence in his abilities. As Bilbie described it: "The frame was a box section underslung beneath the rear axle. The front suspension was based on the prototype vehicle A40 and A90 units. The steering was ours, and we had a problem with that mainly because we were using off-the-shelf components. We revised the damper [shock absorber] system and changed the steering and made the thing handle very very well."

John Thompson Motor Pressings built two prototype chassis. After the first arrived at the Healey works at The Cape, Warwick, it was quickly converted into a running test bed. The A90 engine was installed with a special inlet manifold using two SU carburetors that increased output to 90 hp. The drive train and suspension were Austin components, and the brakes were 10-in Girling drums. Two seats were bolted on, and the chassis was ready to be tested.

"We road tested the cars by driving them on the roads," Geoff Healey remembered.

We drove them up the curbs and on the banks and everything and really made the suspension work and tried everything. You would find the roughest piece of road for testing. There was the MIRA test track, but that was just beginning to be operational. There was no speed restriction on the main roads. You could do whatever the car wanted to do. That helped a lot.

The suspension was based on the conventional Austin components which were used in a very similar manner. So apart from getting the spring rates and shock absorber rates right, it was more or less as used by Austin. It was a suspension that was used on a much heavier motor car, so we didn't need to beef it up too much. We did need to fine tune it to suit our conditions.

Testing of the prototype showed that the overall gear ratios were too low. A Laycock overdrive was fitted, which seemed to be the perfect solution to the problem. Still, first gear was best used for pulling tree stumps, while second gear was a more practical first gear. So first gear in the four-speed A90 gearbox was simply blocked out, yielding a three-speed with overdrive.

Donald wanted to have some sort of official road test published before the car was exhibited at the Earls Court Motor Show in October 1952. "Preparatory to handing it over to the Press, we got it ready for our own high-speed testing," he wrote.

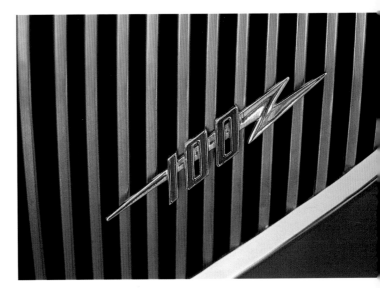

The original grille badge was a simple design. Dave Gooley photo

The 100 has a simple interior and dash that can be dressed up with two-tone seats. The ammeter at right is an aftermarket item.

We took it over to the Jabekke Highway in Belgium, where I managed to do more than 110 mph quite comfortably. Confident, now, that it was not only a pretty car but had performance, too, I arranged with Basil Cardew, of the *Daily Express*, to carry out a short road-test and report on it in his paper. He gave the car a wonderful write-up which, appearing in one of the leading dailies on the opening day of the show, proved invaluable to us–and it provided something of a "scoop" for Basil, as things turned out.

John Bolster of *Autosport* was along on the Jabbeke test and pronounced the Healey Hundred a "very fast everyday road car, of superior refinement, and with exceptionally fine handling qualities." He added that the Healey was "the most important new model that we have seen for some time."

Because it was a late entry, the Healey was given a less-then-ideal exhibit spot at the show. And because Donald still wasn't sure about the shape of the grille, he positioned it so the grille was partially hidden. Still, with its ice-blue paint and Dunlop wire wheels, the car was beautiful. Healey had a price of £850 on the car.

Leonard Lord noticed the car on the day before the show opened. He told Donald that he wanted the car to go into production under Austin's aegis. Overnight the "Healey Hundred" became the "Austin-Healey 100," and Gerry Coker was put to work designing a new badge for the car. Lord also lowered the price of the car to £750.

Donald wrote in his autobiography:

Sir Leonard asked me to go along to his hotel that evening so that we could have a chat in private and perhaps come to an agreement over what we might be able to do with it as a joint effort. "If we can come to some sort of gentleman's agreement," he said, "we can build probably 200 cars a week at Longbridge, whereas at best you can't do more than twenty cars a week at Warwick. It will be a better deal for you financially, and it will suit us well to have a car that'll carry our name into the sporting field."

That evening, after a few hours talking, we reached an agreement. Sir Leonard would take on the manufacture of the cars at the Austin works, paying me a small royalty on each car for the work

Gerry Coker's design for the Austin-Healey 100 profile exhibited his passion for Italian styling.

Detail shot of construction of the streamliner, showing the elongated tail and the curved fin. Gerry Coker photo

we'd done and would still have to do. I insisted that the car went through unchanged, except for the radiator grille and one or two small modifications Geoff made to cater to the American market.

But there were two other sports cars also being developed almost concurrently with the Healey Hundred. Lord Nuffield (William Morris) asked Syd Enever of MG to prepare a design proposal based on the streamlined 1951 MG TD special. This car would emerge several years later as the MGA. And Leonard Lord asked Jensen Motors to produce a replacement for the Austin A40 Sports, which Jensen had already built under contract. Eric Neale designed a sleek car, and a prototype was built, but it wasn't ready for the opening of the show.

Geoffrey Healey, however, discounts the other two efforts. "If you had seen the other cars you'd realize there wasn't any competition," he said in a 1994 interview. "The Jensen was a dreadful thing that came along later. And I think the MG was only mentioned because they put the A90 engine in a cheapened version of their open-wheel car."

What was most important about Lord's acceptance of the Healey and the sudden infusion of money into the fifteen to twenty-five person company, according to Bilbie, was that modifications could be made to the prototype to make it the car everyone had wanted it to be in the first place.

"The first thing we did was revise the steering because we had the money and the power to be able to tell these people that we wanted the best box, not just what they had on the shelf," Bilbie said. "We were able to move the steering box back on the front suspension, which made it a lot safer. On the prototype the steering was way out on outriggers on the front which was almost the second thing you hit if you hit anything."

The front suspension incorporated double wishbones with the top wishbone, a lever-action shock absorber, coil springs, and a normal bottom link. "We figured on using the standard A40 suspension on the prototype, but then we improved the material and increased the bearing sizes," Bilbie added. They also improved the front drum brakes.

"It was certainly a more rigid assembly," Bilbie said. "Actually the suspension did the work, it wasn't the chassis that did the work."

In the rear were semi-elliptic springs and lever-action shock absorbers.

The Austin-Healey 100 was assigned model code BN1. The "B" denoted an Austin engine of between 2,000 and 3,000 cc. The engine in the Healey, of course, was the 2,660 cc unit from the A90. The "N" denoted a two-seater. Later designations of "T" referred to a four-seater and "J" to a convertible. The number "1" merely indicated that the BN1 was the first of a series that would eventually continue to the BJ8.

Jensen Motor Company was assigned the job of building the bodies for the Austin-Healey and retained that contract until the last 3000 Mark III. Jensen was a small family-owned company in West Bromwich, formed in 1934, that had succeeded in building custom-designed versions of mundane production cars. After World War II, the company began production of its own 541 and Chrysler-powered C-V8. But sales of this big car weren't large, and Jensen took to building bodies for other manufacturers, primarily Austin. Because the Jensen brothers were friendly with Donald Healey, he acted as intermediary, and Jensen was awarded the contract to make the bodies. Production began in May 1953. Meanwhile, the Healey company was busy making twenty-five pre-production cars. "The

bodies came over in paint, and we did all the mechanical installations and trim," Barry Bilbie remembers. "That was to get them out to the States and generally get them into the public for publicity purposes."

Donald Healey took six of the first batch to the United States and shipped them to Austin dealers in various parts of the country, from New York to San Francisco. The car was first shown in the United States at the Sebring Twelve-Hour Grand Prix of Endurance in March 1953, but it was not raced. Next it went to the World's Fair in Miami, where it won the premier award as the best car in the show. In April, the car was on display at the New York Auto Show where it won another premier award.

The Autocar's reporter commented on the Healey's appearance at the New York show: "Focal point of the Austin exhibits is the new Austin-Healey 100, gyrating slowly so that the eye may feast on its sleek lines, fine detail finish, and attractive metallic blue paintwork. At under $3,000 there will doubtless be long queues of enthusiasts forming up at daybreak with the cash in their perspiring little palms."

In America

Austin issued a press release, dated March 31, 1953, announcing the "Austin Healey 100" (sic). The release read:

> Healey's greatest triumph of achievement for the sports car enthusiasts is the sleek and speedy Austin-Healey Hundred, with its matchless beauty of design and performance, manufactured by the Austin Motor Company, Ltd., (England). It was shown at the British Motor Show in 1952 where it created a sensation. Mr. Healey has taken the car on a 10,000-mile tour of the country, testing it on all types of terrain, weather conditions, and climates.
>
> It is especially designed for the American market, being the first British sports car with the high power to weight ratio desirable in this country. It will accelerate from a standstill to 60 miles per hour in 11 seconds. It is especially suitable for long distance touring, being fitted with cold weather equipment and possessing ample luggage space. It has the famous A90 engine, with a three-speed transmission, combined with an overdrive which can be used automatically or hand controlled at will. It is also fitted with Rudge Whitworth-type wire wheels and has a unique patented folding screen which has not been previously used.

The Austin-Healey will market in the United States at our coastal ports of entry for $2985.00 fully equipped, including wire wheels, overdrive, heater, and tonneau cover. The price also includes all duties and federal taxes.

Road & Track's analysis of the Austin-Healey 100 was effusive, as was the analysis of most of the automotive press of the time. Publisher John Bond, who reviewed the "Healey Hundred" for *R&T*, wrote, "Any new sports car with the clean modern lines of the new Austin-Healey Hundred would get attention. A new sports car with a top speed of 110 mph and acceleration to match would deserve attention. But when you combine these qualities of appearance and real performance with a price of just over $3,000, the tremendous interest aroused by this new Healey is understandable."

Bond's review further stated that the *R&T* staff was able to reach a top speed of 110 mph, accelerate from 0 to 60 mph in 10.5 sec, accelerate to 80 mph in 20 sec, and to 100 mph in just 37.2 sec. The Healey Hundred covered the quarter mile in 18 sec. Yes, here was a new performer for the American market.

A later *Road & Track* review called the 100 "a perfect example of fairly 'ordinary' components assembled together in such an ingenious manner that the results are almost unbelievable." This later test achieved a top speed of 106.0 mph "in full touring trim" but posted a slightly slower 0 to 60 mph time of 11.7 sec. List price was quoted at $2,985.

Specification-wise, the BN1 had a 90 in wheelbase and was 146 in long overall, with a front track of 48.8 in and a rear track of 49.5 in. The 2,660 cc Austin engine was rated at 90 hp at 4,000 rpm with a compression ration of 7.5:1. The BN1 had a curb weight of 2,150 lb and a *Road & Track* test weight of 2,470 pounds with 51 percent of its weight on the rear wheels. Tire size was a narrow (by today's standards) 5.90x15, the equivalent of a modern 150/78R15 radial. But these were bias-ply tires. Instruments consisted of a

The finished streamliner. This version of the basic Healey was fitted with a 224 hp supercharged 100S engine. Donald Healey drove the car at 192.74 mph over the flying kilometer at Bonneville, while Carroll Shelby set a one-hour record of 157.62 mph in the car. Gerry Coker photo

Here's a British Racing Green Austin-Healey on a California road. Dave Gooley photo

speedometer, tachometer, ammeter, oil pressure, and water temperature gauges.

After the first twenty-five cars were built at Warwick, Longbridge in Birmingham built a pre-production run of 100 cars. Barry Bilbie and Roger Menadue, who was chief experimental engineer, traveled from Warwick to Birmingham to assist in getting production started. "It was a little bit frustrating," Bilbie remembered:

At Warwick we had only a few people and if you wanted a job done you did it yourself. And it was not unusual for us designers to be under the vehicle with a spanner doing tugs and snubs.

At Longbridge it was slightly different. They were a very strong union company. We were warned right from the beginning that in no way whatsoever were we to pick up a spanner or any tool whatever. So you can imagine how frustrating it was for Roger and me to have to point to a particular thing and tell someone it has to go over there and it has to be fitted there. And we thought, "Oh hell, I can do this bloody job myself in less time."

But the workers at Longbridge were enthusiastic about the Austin-Healey. The line manager was Lord Austin's brother, Alan, who had worked with his brother, the founder of the company, in the 1920s. Bilbie said he often talked with him and their conversations spanned generations.

"He was getting on in years," Roger Menadue remembered, "so they put him in charge of the Austin-Healey venture. I worked with him showing him how the Austin-Healey went together, and we had a wonderful time."

"We were very fortunate with the Hundred," Menadue continued. "When it went to America it caught on in such a way that we were the biggest dollar earner in the [British] car industry in America for four years. And of course the British banks and the government were delighted. Eventually we were overtaken by Jaguar."

Competition

Longbridge handled Austin-Healey production, but the Warwick facility was home to all the competition cars. "From the first car I was what you would call the chief of the experimental department," Menadue said. "I did all the prototypes, right through the history of the Healey company. And the race cars–the rally cars in the earlier days–before it became too much for us, and we turned the rally stuff over to MG in Abingdon."

The first official competition event for the Hundred was the Lyons-Charbonnieres Rally. Donald loaned one of the early prototypes to Peter Reece and Gregor Grant. But the team encountered a pothole at high speed which broke off one of the rear shock absorbers. Reece and Grant finished the rally but were unplaced.

Two cars were entered in the 1953 Mille Miglia, but both retired with throttle linkage problems. Johnny Lockett and Jock Reid were able to make it to twenty miles from the finish before retiring, though.

In June 1953, Healey entered two cars at Le Mans. Despite an attack of food poisoning that beset all the team members and an accident with one of the cars the night before the race, both cars finished with no problems. Johnny Lockett and Maurice Gatsonides finished twelfth behind a Nash-Healey, with Marcel Becquart and Gordon Wilkins fourteenth.

The large tachometer and speedometer located directly in front of the driver supply all the pertinent information. The basic layout of the instrument panel would remain unchanged until 1964 and the introduction of the 3000.

Donald Healey's personal Austin-Healey 100 coupe parked in front of his house. According to Gerry Coker, this was one of the few cars that Donald kept for more *than a few days. It was a design he really liked.* Gerry Coker photo

Geoffrey and his wife Margot took one of the rally cars on their honeymoon after an event. Margot worked for a travel agent and was able to arrange for accommodations, and Geoffrey continued testing the rally car along the way.

The most astounding of the Healey's first-year successes came on Utah's Bonneville Salt Flats. In September 1953, a team of drivers captured a pocketful of speed records in a pair of Austin-Healeys. A specially tuned car achieved a top speed of 146.626 mph on a two-way run. The stock car took all American stock car records from five to 3,000 miles and from one to 24 hours and averaged 21 mpg to boot. Drivers for the attempts were Donald Healey, George Eyston, actor Jackie Cooper, Roy Jackson-Moore, and John Gordon Bennett.

BN2

The BN1 stayed in production for two years and five months, during which time 10,688 cars were built. It was replaced in August 1955 by the BN2, which used the same 2,660 cc engine but incorporated a true four-speed transmission with overdrive on third and fourth and hypoid gears in the rear axle. "The hypoid axle was certainly an advantage as far as we were concerned," Barry Bilbie said. "It was a better axle altogether, and was more rigid."

In fact, Bilbie rates the BN2 as his favorite among all the Big Healeys. "At that time it was the only vehicle around of that type," he said. "There were other vehicles but they were a lot more expensive. This car was selling for $3,000 in the States, which was £750 in England. The Jaguar, I think at that time, was another £100."

Over the course of one year's production (August 1955 to August 1956), BMC Longbridge built 3,924 BN2 Austin-Healey Hundreds. The BN2 would be succeeded by the BN4, also known as the 100-6. But a pair of non-standard Austin-Healeys would fit between the BN2 and BN4 in the long history of the marque; the 100S and 100M.

The 100's Austin engine. Leonard Lord of BMC gave Healey a 2,660 cc inline four-cylinder engine to use for the "Healey Hundred" prototype. After Lord saw the car at the London Motor Show, he agreed to build the car. The Austin engine developed 90 hp at 4,000 rpm. Since it was originally designed for trucks, it was more than powerful enough for a sports car.

In the Driver's Seat

Jerry Smith on his first car, an Austin-Healey 100–4.

It was a great, great car to drive. The greatest car I ever owned. But a lot of things came into play around the time I owned that car. I was going to the University of Montana when I bought it used in 1956. The original owner bought it in England. He was a rancher, and the car only had 2,400 miles on it. When he was driving to the ranch he knocked holes in the oil pan, so he had a steel covering on the bottom. This led to overheating. It was the fourth sports car in Montana. I drove it to San Francisco and met my wife-to-be there. Both Leigh and I did a lot of autocrossing and competition with that car. The Healey had a 2,600 cc engine. In the old days there were over- and under-2,500 cc racing classes, so we had to race with the big cars—very early Corvettes, Jaguars, and such. My wife was consistently among the best three times of the day, *male or female*. There was one very well-to-do woman in a black Porsche 356 who had trouble dealing with this.

We have fond memories of the Healey. Everything, that is, except the stupid fuel pump. There was a flap between the seats. We always carried a 10- or 12-in wrench with us. When the fuel pump acted up, we'd lift the flap, give the pump a couple of whacks, and get it going again.

We drove the car from San Francisco to Oregon quite often. Leigh was from Oregon. So when we drove it in the winter, it was cold with the flap up. Let me add about the heater. It could melt the polish off your shoes in fourteen seconds. When you needed it, the heat was there, but you had to turn it off.

The car had a planetary gear system. It was three speeds forward with overdrive on the top two gears, which gave five speeds. With the 100S, they freed up first gear from the four-speed gearbox.

The car was British Racing Green; the only BRG Healey in California at the time. To most of the people into British cars, BRG was okay. You had *the* car.

We kept the car four years. I bought it in 1956 for $2,400 and drove it four years. A guy who also parked where I parked had a '55 Porsche 356 coupe that he was using as a business car and writing off. When my wife had an accident with the Healey, I told him that if he ever wanted to sell the Porsche, I'd be interested. He sold it to me on the spot for $1,800. I sold the Healey for $1,700 and change and bought the Porsche. I drove the Porsche for two years and sold it for $900 cash plus a 1948 Mark IV Jaguar and a 1952 Plymouth. So for all our sports car years we had essentially zero expense. It was an incredible era to live in. We have never owned another sports car.

Bob Tebbenhoff

In 1963, Bob Tebbenhoff's father bought a 1955 Austin-Healey 100, a BN1. It was one of many cars the elder Tebbenhoff owned, but it was the one that fascinated his son the most. The car remained in the family, and when Bob's computer application company grew to a point where there was a need for a warehouse, Bob made sure that the warehouse was big enough to store the Healey. Restoration began in 1991.

"I had been working on the car and still had some work to do but it was driveable. My father came over and we couldn't start the car. My ten-year-old son Jason kept bothering us, but we ignored him.

Finally, after much frustration, my father said he was going to go home and we'd work out the problem at another time. Jason said, 'Dad, will you listen to me now?' So we did. He said, 'The distributor with the four black wires going to the spark plugs and the white wire going to the coil is where you had problems before. Maybe if you checked the coil wire the car will start.'

We did, and the car started. Since then, the car has been part of his growing-up project."

The Austin-Healey looks good no matter what the back-ground is. Donald Healey often traveled to California when he was in the United States, and it's appropriate that California is the location of some of the more active Healey clubs today. Dave Gooley photo

Chapter 3

100S and 100M

Allowing the Healey works to tend to the competition side of the program was like giving a kid the key to the candy store. It allowed Donald, Geoffrey, and Roger Menadue certain liberties that they were quick to take advantage of. A much-modified 100 (actually an early prototype of a new model, the 100S) was entered at Sebring in March 1954. Lance Macklin and George Huntoon drove the car to third place overall behind Stirling Moss and Bill Lloyd in an OSCA and Porfirio Rubirosa and Gino Valenzano in a Lancia. This was an outstanding finish for a new car. They took the 3-ltr class win by twenty-two laps over a Brooks Stevens Excalibur.

The Sebring cars used a Harry Weslake-designed head with four ports that helped the Austin four-banger develop around 130 hp. This was tied to a David Brown close-ratio four-speed gearbox. Dunlop disc brakes were installed at all four corners for better stopping.

According to Peter Browning in *Safety Fast*, (the MG Car Club and Austin-Healey Club magazine) inside the last hour Macklin was in third place with a good chance at finishing higher or even winning the race outright: "Moss was driving with practically no brakes, while the Lancia was a

Since the 100M was built to give the production car buyer something close to the performance of the 100S, many owners didn't race them, but used them as simply better-performing road Healeys. British Racing Green was on the designer's pallet, as it was for all British sports cars of the 1950s and 1960s. Dave Gooley photo

The first 100S being tested at Gaydon Royal Air Force Base on a Sunday morning just prior to going over to Bonneville, Utah, to break some records. Donald Healey is driving. Behind the car, from left: Leonard Lord, John Rich, BMC Chief Engineer Geoff Healey, BMC Technicians Alec Marshall and W. Reid, Roger Menadue. Roger Menadue photo

very tired machine and its driver far from experienced. As the race drew to a close, Macklin made a last-minute attempt to bring the Austin-Healey through into the lead, but after nearly twelve hours of racing, this final spurt proved too much for the '100S,' and a rocker arm fractured. With the Austin-Healey running unsteadily on three cylinders, Macklin was forced to drop back and be content with a secure third place."

But the fun of the race for Macklin (who called Sebring a "dismal race") was the trip down.

He and team manager Mort Morris Goodall took a boat to New York and picked up their car there. Donald Healey told them to keep the revs below 3,500 for the beginning of the trip as it was a new engine.

This they did, but that equated to about 70 mph, which was still over the speed limit for the New Jersey Turnpike. The state trooper who pulled them over first looked into the left side of the car, but Goodall told them he wasn't the driver. When the Trooper came over to Macklin's side, he had

Jack Breskovich's Austin-Healey 100S leads an A.C. Ace-Bristol and another 100S in a Cal Club regional at the Los Angeles County Fairgrounds in 1959. Bob Tronolone photo

A 100S racing in England. The 100S differed from the 100M (and base 100) by its two-tone paint, oval radiator grille, and light aluminum body. The 100S provided amateur racers with a fast, safe car that was relatively inexpensive.

both revolvers out and ordered both men out of the car. They paid "some large sum of money" and continued on their way.

In North Carolina, they were on a straight stretch of road with nothing in sight and decided to open up the engine. Macklin took the Austin-Healey up to about 100 mph and stayed there for about 100 miles. They slowed to go through a town and discovered they were being followed again. The Sheriff said, "Gee that's a little whizzer you've got there. I've been doing 100 mph for the last twenty-five miles and couldn't catch you."

Here's a 100M at the start of California's Little Mille Miglia. The event is a jaunt around the state, primarily for older sports cars, and is closer to a rally than a race. Dave Gooley photo

"They fined me some colossal sum, and it was only because I was able to produce my passport and prove I'd only just arrived in the States a few days before and they didn't put me in jail," Macklin said in a later interview. "By the time we got to Sebring, Donald said that the next time he reckoned it would be cheaper to fly the car out."

After the successful Sebring race, Healey Motors decided to build a small number of similar cars at Warwick. They would be designated 100S (for Sebring). With the support of Austin, a prototype was built in late 1954. According to Geoff Healey: "The basis was the standard 100 body shell and chassis frame. John Thompson modified the chassis frames, incorporating various strengthening gussets and brackets for the larger DAS10 rear [shock absorbers]. The frame was delivered to Jensen, who built the all-aluminum bodies on to it. The aluminum panels were produced on standard tools. Gerry Coker restyled the front end to include a smaller, distinctive grille and designed a neat per-

spex [plastic] screen. No provision was made for hood or side windows, although several owners later fitted the standard 100 equipment."

To make the cars more race-ready, Dunlop disc brakes with chromium-plated steel rotors and calipers and round pads were installed. Twenty-gallon fuel tanks were also added with quick-release filler caps, giving the 100S eight more gallons over the standard 100 model. Fuel reached the engine through twin SU fuel pumps and two 1-3/4-in SU HD6 carburetors.

In 1953, a special test car, which was a precursor of the 100S, was prepared to attack some race records at the Bonneville Salt Flats. The idea was to set some records at a time that would coincide with the arrival of the cars at American

Next page
The 100M was a variation of the 100 that gave owners near-100S performance.

dealers. Gerry Coker described the development of the streamliner chassis.

Don came in and said he was thinking of trying to set some speed records. He said he'd like to use the 100 shape, and he told me to see what I could come up with. It was the usual stuff—see what you can come up with, see you next week.

I cut the nose off at the center line of the front wheel and just shaped it to what I thought was a nice-looking shape. I made a clay model, about one foot long and took it to Armstrong-Whitworth Aircraft Company and they put it in their wind tunnel and tested it. They quoted a speed of something like 198 mph.

Don decided it was too expensive to make that car, but we found out we could make the same shape by using the Healey shell. So that's what we did.

The shape looked alright without the fin, but talking to Don about it I said I thought it would look more dramatic if it had a dorsal fin on it. I showed him a sketch I had done. We had no idea if it would do any good at all. He was worried about a side wind catching it, which is why it was cut down so. I made as small a fin as possible so it wasn't affected by any side wind when he was doing his 200 mph run.

Geoff organized the building of the special test car, which included an engine modified by Austin that had a head based on Harry Weslake's four-port design that would be used in the 100S. They also brought along a stock car to take a shot at some production records as well. In preliminary tests on the Salt Flats, the stock car lapped the 10-mile circle at 111 mph while the Special Test car got up to 140 mph.

Between September 9 and September 16, 1953, the two cars set a number of records from 1–kilometer to thirty hours. Donald Healey drove the cars for many of these records, including the 1–kilometer and 1-mile flying start in the Special Test Car, and records up to ten miles for the stock car and Special Test Car.

A production line was set up at Warwick, and a total of fifty-five or fifty-six cars were built to 100S specifications. But they weren't dealing with exotic mechanicals. "If you looked at our engines, they were all obsolete when we took them," Roger Menadue said.

With the 100S we had the ordinary Austin engine, which was about the same size as the Riley

The slightly modified Austin-Healey 100 engine used in the 100M, showing the altered air box feeding the carburetors. The 100M gave improved performance, but it was no 100S.

and performed about the same as the Riley. We thought that if we could develop an aluminum head and alter the breathing and so forth, it would perform a bit better. So we got Harry Weslake, the engine specialist, to design a head for it.

We took the BN1 and put this engine in there. And if you look at it, the car has the same grille and everything as the BN1. And we raced it at Sebring.

We made about fifty-six. We made about six or seven special cars in my department. And then Donald asked if we could make a run of fifty because various people wanted them. In all, there were about fifty-six cars with 100S engines that were built. That included a coupe which Donald had as his personal car.

Donald's coupe turned out to be his favorite. It was a standard BN1 with an aluminum top added to it, and it was designed by Gerry Coker. When Healey first acquired the car, it was powered by the standard A90 engine. But after a few weeks, he asked Menadue to put a 100S engine in the car. "We thought it would go like stink then," Menadue said recently. "It should [have been] quicker than the open cars because it was more streamlined and closed in, instead of an open car which would have more drag."

The coupe was the only car Donald kept for any length of time, according to Menadue. Normally, he would take a car for a few days and then turn it over to someone else.

Most bodies were painted white, according to Geoff Healey, with a blue bottom and sides. Since these colors "just happened" to be the American racing colors, there was no doubt as to the intended destination of the cars. Unfortunately, the price of the cars was chosen to give a minimum profit, but the Austin organization in the United States added a huge mark-up to fund its racing program. *Road & Track* quoted a list price of $4,995 in its September 1955 test.

Road & Track's test report said the 100S was from the "extremist" school of thought, where someone will give up anything and everything for the goal of maximum performance with minimum weight. Their 100S had a test weight of 2,310 lb versus 2,470 lb for the stock 100. Top speed was 120 mph, and the 100S went from 0 to 60 mph in 7.8 sec (versus 11.7 for the stock car) and from 0-100 mph in 24.4 sec (versus over 40 sec for the base 100).

One feature the 100S donated to future big Austin-Healeys was the oval grille. The triangular grille and its variations had served Donald Healey well from the days of his first Westlands-bodied roadster. But with the introduction of the 100S, it was felt that a new, more modern grille was in order. Gerry Coker designed the grille, which finally satisfied his desire for a clean shape.

Panamericana

Carroll Shelby also took part in the record-breaking runs at the Bonneville Salt Flats. Shelby was also one of the drivers in one of the Austin-Healey 100Ss entered in the last Panamericana Road Race in Mexico in November 1954. Shelby remembered that race, which wasn't one of his career highlights: "The race was the nearest thing this side of the Atlantic we've ever had to the Mille Miglia or the Targa Florio. It was a paved road, all the way from Tuxola to Juarez. It was only a little old hogback paved road, but it was paved. It wasn't excellent. But you could run along on the straightaways 150 mph. We went through the desert, too. Hell, you had 2,000 miles of desert in 2,500 miles of racing."

Shelby, co-driving with Roy Jackson-Moore, was up to fourth overall after the first leg. "I was ahead of all the Lincolns except one and fourth behind Phil Hill and Umberto Maglioli when I [screwed] up and lost it," Shelby remembered. "I just screwed up. I came into a negative camber curve and I was just going too fast."

"I started racing with those big Lincolns and was really givin' 'em hell," he wrote in his autobiography. "I had just gotten by Vukovich and Verne Houle and taken off after Crawford when I came around a corner a little too fast and suddenly there was a big rock standing in the way. The rock never batted an eyelash but I went end-over-end four or five times."

The 100M also wore a slightly modified "100" grille slash. Dave Gooley photo

Fortunately, Jackson-Moore had abandoned the car and was waiting at the next checkpoint for his turn to drive. A kilometer marker-stone went into the passenger side of the Healey during Shelby's cartwheel. In addition, the wheels on the right side of the car were torn off. When the natives picked him up, Shelby had cuts and bruises and a broken elbow. They eased his pain with a couple of bottles of Mexican beer. Then "two school girls from Brooklyn," according to Shelby, stopped by and added some brandy to the pain killer. By the time the ambulance came to pick Shelby up, he was almost unconscious.

There were other problems for Shelby and the Healeys in leaving Mexico. It seemed the authorities (at least at that time) insisted that a car leaving the country must be the same as the one entering. But the Healey had lost two wheels in the accident. Fortunately, a cooperative Healey owner donated two wheels which allowed the team to return to the United States and Shelby to head home to Dallas and his family orthopedic surgeon.

Sebring

With the 100S virtually named for the Sebring race, the 1955 Sebring 12-Hour Grand Prix of Endurance in March was an important venue. Stirling Moss and Lance Macklin were assigned the official works entry, but there were seven 100S cars entered in the race. Five completed it, along with two other 100 models.

Peter Browning, in his series "From Perranporth to Abingdon" in *Safety Fast*, wrote that Moss, being the master of the Le Mans start, gave

Danny Stephens' Austin-Healey 100M (as identified by the original race program) battles with a Triumph at the *L.A. County Fairgrounds parking lot track in 1960.* Bob Tronolone photo

the team a good beginning in the race and kept the car up with the leading Jaguars and Ferraris during the early hours. Actor Jackie Cooper was also among the top twelve cars and was lapping consistently at 81 mph. Moss and Macklin remained among the top ten during the first half of the race. Then, Browning writes:

After eight hours' racing, Moss and Macklin had brought the Austin-Healey up to sixth place behind the leading D-Type Jaguar, two Ferraris, and two Maseratis. Electrical trouble and an excursion into a sand bank delayed the Cooper/Jackson-Moore 100S, so they trailed several laps in arrears. The race drew to a close with no change amongst the leaders; Moss and Macklin maintaining their very creditable sixth place overall. More significant was the fact that the Austin-Healeys had made it a 1-2-3 victory in the series production class. With five out of the seven cars finishing to dominate their class, the '100S' had put up a convincing demonstration on the doorstep of the American market.

Moss and Macklin's sixth place car was six laps behind the winners and only one lap behind the fifth-place Ferrari of Taruffi and Schell.

Ship and Shore Motors of West Palm Beach had entered one of the other 100S racers. With George Huntoon and Ship and Shore service man Phil Stiles driving, the car finished eleventh. It was then driven back to the dealership. According to Geoff Healey, the car's only failing came when the gear selector broke on the trip back.

Le Mans

The only time the 100S ran at Le Mans was in the fateful year of 1955. Roger Menadue believes that surprise over the performance of the 100S may have been a contributing factor in the Pierre Levegh Mercedes crash that killed more than eighty people. "Levegh hit our car on the circuit and it was a disaster," Menadue remembers.

I heard Mike Hawthorne say to Lance Macklin after the crash, "I never realized you were going so fast, Lance." I think poor Mike misjudged the speed. He thought there was an ordinary Healey out there which had a top speed of about 120.

Instead of that there was this 100S out there–it was the first time it had ever appeared at Le Mans–and that damned thing was going down the Mulsanne Straight at 150! I think Mike thought that he had plenty of time to pass our Healey and get in front of it and get into the pits. While we were coming up into the pits probably at least at 120 or 130, Mike passed us and immediately pulled across Lance's bow with his brakes on, going down through the gears. So Lance had no alternative but to brake hard himself and get out into the faster part of the circuit. Levegh was driving the third Mercedes and was behind Lance. When Lance pulled out, Levegh hit him and went out of control. But a lot of people fail to realize that they were on the same lap, and Lance was ahead of Levegh.

The accident and resulting inquiry and its affect on the sport kept the Austin-Healey team away from Le Mans for several years.

Sardi with his 100S on the race track. Walt Hansgen suggested the additional grille to Sardi because he didn't think the radiator was getting enough air. Vincent Sardi collection

Stirling Moss drove a 100S in the 1955 Nassau race, without success. "Anybody who drives a Healey in a race is either crazy or bloody good," Moss said. "I raced that Healey at Nassau, and the top wishbone broke. It was a bumpy course, but they still shouldn't break. But Donald Healey was such a nice guy that you'd drive anything for him."

Lance Macklin said he thought the 100S "was a tough, reliable motor car, and it was about the only car that you could start off in something like the Mille Miglia or Pan-Americana and be pretty sure to finish.

Amateurs at the Wheel

The 100S proved to be a very popular car among amateur racers as well as professionals. One of the amateurs was noted restaurateur Vincent Sardi, who drove a 100S when it first came out. Sardi's 100S was his fifth race car, even though, as he says, he started racing late in life.

Sardi began racing with a Jaguar XK120M in 1952, then switched to an Alfa Romeo. But the Alfa kept breaking—once the driveshaft broke when Sardi was leading a race at Virginia International Raceway. So Sardi sold the Alfa and bought a Healey. He decided to retire after a year, but then un-retired and bought a Jaguar coupe. Then Austin-Healey came out with the 100S and Sardi was sold. "I really enjoyed that car," he said. "It was fun to drive. I did very well with it. I always placed either second or third. Occasionally I would win. In those days I just didn't have the time. For example, when Jackie Cooper and I were both racing a 100S and he was in a show, we'd go up to Lime Rock in the morning and practice, come back, and he'd do his show, and I'd work at the restaurant. The next day we'd go up and race, come back and do the show and work at the restaurant. So I really didn't have the time to put into it that you really have to if you're going to be consistently a winner."

Sardi's 100S was modified by Walt Hansgen, who put an extra grille in the front to increase cooling. Sardi remembered, "Walt thought that since we were running on short courses without very long stretches—Lime Rock, Thompson, etc.—he thought we should get more air into the oil cooler. So he put that in. It was not for appearance. I used to drive the car on the street, and in traffic you need more cooling."

Many drivers in that era would drive their cars to the races, take off the mufflers and tape over the headlights so they wouldn't break, and go racing. Sardi, in fact, wanted to have a requirement for straight-through exhausts because part of the fun of racing is the noise, and he felt cars that ran with mufflers on didn't make enough noise.

100M

With the success of the 100S, there were more customers for the car than there were cars. There was a finite number of Weslake heads available for the four-cylinder Austin engine (fifty-five

Sardi's restaurant in New York City is famed for is caricatures. Here's a caricature of owner Vincent Sardi racing his 100S. Vincent Sardi photo

"It was a frightening car to drive in the wet—it certainly oversteered rather violently—and it was difficult to keep on the road at 130 to 140 on those slippery Italian roads. It was a car that always amazed me. Considering that it was only an old taxi engine it was remarkable how fast it could be made to go."

This angle shows the main exterior difference between the 100 and 100M: the bonnet strap and louvered hood.

to fifty-seven, depending on your source) and a limited number of lightweight bodies as well. Austin-Healey's solution was to build a group of cars with an accessory package. These cars were called 100M (for Le Mans, or modified) and a small production number was built on the normal Austin-Healey production line at Longbridge. There were no production numbers for the 100M modifications because of the manner of manufacture. The basis for the 100M was the modifications used on the 1953 Le Mans Austin-Healey, which was the competition debut of the BN1.

Among the 100M engine modifications were larger (1-3/4 in) SU carburetors, higher compression (8.1:1) pistons, larger inlet manifolds, and the Le Mans camshaft, which gave longer opening periods and greater valve lift. A steel cylinder-head gasket was also used. In addition, a special cold air box supplied air to the carburetors. Total modifications to the engine raised output to 110 hp.

The suspension was firmed up with a larger diameter front antiroll bar and stiffer shock absorber settings.

From the outside, you could recognize a 100M by the louvered hood secured by a leather strap, which mimicked the Le Mans cars. The car also carried the distinctive blue-and-white two-tone paint scheme of the 100S.

Austin-Healey claimed 110 hp at 4,500 rpm for the 100M engine, versus 90 hp at 4,000 rpm for

The 100M had a dash that was identical to the 100. This made sense, since the only modifications to the base 100 were under the hood, where engine modifications increased the power output to 110 hp.

Bob Eshelman's 100M is equipped with a full array of aftermarket accessories, including fog lights and headlight guards. The chrome wire wheels help complete the restoration.

the standard BN1/2 100. Torque, however was curiously lower (143 lb-ft at 2,600 rpm versus 144 lb-ft at 2,000 rpm). Performance was marginally better than that of a standard 100, with a claimed top speed of 118 mph versus 111 for the 100 (with the windshield lowered), a 0 to 60 mph time of 10.0 sec (versus 10.3 sec), and a standing quarter mile of 17.2 sec (versus 17.5 sec).

In general, however, the 100M was not raced as successfully as the 100S because of the obvious difference in performance based on the engine and weight of the car. But it did satisfy customers who wanted a higher level of performance than the standard 100 offered.

Chapter 4

100-6

Roger Menadue said one of the problems Healey cars suffered throughout their lifetimes was their engines. They were always obsolete, and Healey had to make do with whatever other manufacturers were willing to sell him. Obviously, these weren't always the best engines to come from those manufacturers, and Healey had to devise innovative ways of making the cars that carried these engines perform better than the ones that carried them originally.

Donald Healey heard that the Austin A90 four-cylinder engine was going out of production. Leonard Lord had initiated a standard engine policy whereby three basic engines would henceforth power all BMC vehicles: the A-series four-cylinder of 850 cc for cars such as the Morris Minor and Austin A30, the B-series of about 1,500 cc for cars like the Austin A50 and MGA sports car, and the C-series six-cylinder of about 2,600 cc for bigger cars like the Austin A90, Wolseley 6/90, and Morris Isis. It was this six-cylinder engine that was proposed for the Austin-Healey.

Although yellow was a color choice for the 100-6, this particular color with the blue seats is a combination that was the choice of the owner and restorer. In profile, the 100-Six exhibits the sleek Austin-Healey lines. The hood bulge, adapted for the longer six-cylinder engine, is barely visible. The folding windshield was abandoned with the 100-Six and later cars, though. The style line is also slightly modified to include a downward sweep behind the front wheel arches.

The cockpit of the 100-6 was enlarged slightly, but the car retained the same dash and instrument panel as its predecessor. The spare tire was still mounted in the cockpit, behind the seats. In later cars it would be relocated to the trunk.

In its prototype form the new six-cylinder developed only 92 hp at 4,500 rpm. However, Geoff and Eddie Maher, an ex-Riley development engineer, were able to increase power output from the 2639 cc engine to 102 bhp at 4,600 rpm with an 8.25:1 compression ratio. But the six still wasn't popular, especially after the glory days of the 100S. Roger Menadue remembers his disappointment with the car.

I never did care for the six to be quite honest. The six, when we got it, wouldn't perform like the four. And that's very discouraging, really, when you bring out a new car. Tom McCahill and all those boys said they never heard of anybody bringing out a car that went slower than the previous one. Not if they were in the sports car business. And of course that's what we did.

Many manufacturers produce sixes that don't perform as well as their fours. Austin was always noted for that. Their side-valve engines were wonderful engines. All the best ones were four cylinders. I remember as a boy when they went over to six-cylinder side-valve engines they started burning valves. They weren't nearly as reliable as their old four.

We were going in a retrograde step from my point of view. I was always trying to get performance out of a car. That was my business.

As with the other cars using the engine, the BN4 used horizontal, side-draft SU carburetors. This would change with the upgraded engine, which used semi-downdraft SU carbs.

Previous page
In one color, the style line is more subtle. The "Parker pen" chrome highlight is installed backwards on this car.

The new engine was connected to the same BMC four-speed transmission that was used on the BN2, with the optional Laycock overdrive. The gearbox drove the rear wheels through the BN2 hypoid rear end, with a different ratio—3.9:1 standard and 4.1:1—for overdrive cars.

Because the engine was also longer, the body had to be lengthened, and the front end had to be redesigned as well. Barry Bilbie remembered the work that was required: "It meant a complete redesign of the front end. The suspension towers were almost the same but the compression struts were changed from a box section to a formed section–shallower–because the engine was so much longer. The suspension was upgraded, too, and we were getting on into even better brakes."

In addition, the radiator was moved forward, and the wheelbase lengthened by 1.66 in. While Geoffrey Healey claimed that the added length made for a more acceptable driveshaft length, in reality the extra length was probably to accommodate the extra two seats stuffed in the boot behind the original two. While the front and rear of the Healey remained basically unchanged, the added length was in the seating area. This meant the doors were lengthened by about 2 in. To make room for the extra seats, the two 6-volt batteries of the BN1 and BN2 were replaced by a single 12-volt battery, which was placed in the trunk behind the passenger seat. Also added to the trunk was the spare tire, which had previously been in the space behind the front seats where those two extra seats

In the official press introduction from importer Hambro Automotive, the Austin-Healey 100-6 was described as being "as rugged and power-packed as it is sleek and beautiful."

A Healey Ice Blue 100-6 with fog lamps fitted. Healey Ice Blue was the color of the first 100 and has always been considered the "standard" Healey color. Many *owners fitted fog lamps for additional lighting, especially in the United States.*

The 100-6 would assume the shape of all Big Healeys to come, with its longer hood to accommodate the extra two cylinders. With Gerry Coker's style line, the Big Healey looks especially attractive in two-tone paint.

now resided. The spare would remain in the trunk, even on the two-seat versions, severely reducing carrying capacity.

The 100-6 retained the oval grille of the 100S, but the vertical chrome strips in the center were replaced by horizontal strips. With a taller and longer engine, a hood scoop was added that would remain with the car for the rest of its life. The wheelbase and overall length of the 100-6 were both increased by 2 in, primarily to accommodate the longer engine.

Restyling at the rear included reflectors incorporated into the body panels and an external fuel filler rather one hidden in the trunk. Wire wheels were now optional, whereas in the BN1 and BN2 they had been standard equipment. The BN4 model was nominally a four-seater, but the rear seats were only useful for two children without legs or an adult if he is a suitcase. Exterior door handles replaced the inside handles that were always a bother, especially if you were carrying packages.

The rear end treatment of the 100-6 was modified from the original 100 with the addition of an extra light on the fenders.

The new model was designated BN4, but what happened to the BN3? According to research reported by David McLavin and Andrew Tipping, the "one and only BN3 was the first Austin-Healey fitted with the 2,639 cc C-Series engine." It was essentially a BN2 100 with a different rear suspension that would have improved ground clearance, according to the authors. In addition, since the engine was longer than the A90, it was mounted on a separate subframe assembly.

The 100-6 was introduced in September 1956, concurrent with the announcement of a new set of records broken by Austin-Healey. These records were set at Bonneville with six-cylinder cars. One car was a conventional BN2 with streamlined body extensions front and rear. Carroll Shelby and Roy Jackson-Moore drove this car for long-distance runs and succeeded in establishing six Class D records, including 500 miles at 153.14 mph and six hours at 145.96 mph.

Shelby enjoyed the record runs. "Really there's nothing to it. You just run around in a big circle or you run down a straight line. The Salt Flats at that time had pretty good quality salt. Now you don't have that anymore. But there wasn't much to it. Oh, at 160 or 170 mph in a circle, once in a while the ass end would wiggle a little bit, but nothing serious.

"When you consider that it was a little, pushrod, cast-iron engine, it was absolutely amazing to accomplish what it did."

The second car prepared for the Bonneville assault was the 1954 streamliner with a 250 hp su-

percharged version of the C-type engine. Donald Healey drove this car, and despite several aborted runs because of supercharger problems, he did manage to get one run in at 203.06 mph, which when averaged with another run enabled him to join the then-exclusive 200 mph Club.

Road & Track tested an early 100-6 fitted with two rear seats. And, as Roger Menadue feared, performance simply wasn't up to the standard set by the 100-4. The list price, as stated in the January 1957 road test, was $3,195.

The engine was rated at 102 hp, some 12 hp more than the four, but the curb weight was listed by *R&T* as 2,480 lb, 330 lb more than the earlier model. Consequently, 0 to 60 mph times for the six-cylinder car were 12.2 sec compared to 11.7 for the four, and the top speed was only marginally improved, from 102 mph to 105 mph.

Road & Track said, in conclusion: "We should admit that we like the 'looks' of the old car better than the new, but this Six has a real potential both in immediate sales and in future develop-

The biggest change from the 100 to the 100-6 was, of course, the BMC "C" engine. It was a 2,639 cc unit rated at 117 hp, twenty-seven more than the original 100.

However, the extra weight of the car made for less spirited performance. With the new engine, the hood now opened from the front rather than the rear.

100-6 identification plate. The new model was designed BN4 (two-plus-two seating arrangement) or BN6 (the two-seater). The engine designation was 26D.

ment towards even more performance." The testers felt that the steering wheel was too close to the chest and too high, but the steering was excellent. The new, larger top received praise for its more graceful look, but the testers said it was a chore to stow properly behind the rear seats. The aluminum-framed side curtains received praise for fitting neatly.

A contemporary evaluation in a British publication called the 100-6 "less 'sports' and more 'GT' than the originals."

One driver who was certainly able to wring the maximum performance out of a 100-6 was "The Racing Dentist," Dr. Dick Thompson of Washington, D.C.

I raced an Austin-Healey 100-6 in 1958. I had been racing Corvettes [in fact, Thompson raced one of the Grand Sport Corvettes at Sebring], but GM backed out of racing in 1957. This car [the 100-6] became available through Manhattan Auto near Washington. Ed Brown took care of the car and took it to the races, and I met him there. I was just the driver. It was a semi-professional arrangement–I got my expenses paid. In those days that was pretty good.

I had driven the Grand Sport. This [the 100-6] was a lower performance car, but it's all relative. My biggest competitor was an AC Bristol which, on paper at least, had a lot more potential. Let's say it was a better effort by all concerned that pro-

duced the wins. Between me and Ed, we got the most out of the car that there was. We beat the AC Bristol in some races, not all of them. The AC Bristol driver was a guy named Harry Carter from Massachusetts.

We just raced it in SCCA Nationals, and we won the championship. I don't recall, offhand, how many races we won, but it was enough to win the championship. And it was mostly on the East Coast.

The Healey was a very honest car. The only drawback to it was that it was a little bit heavy, a little bit ponderous, at least compared to the Bristol. But I was kind of used to that. It didn't have quite the horsepower-to-weight that the Corvette did. I have no idea how much power he got out of it. Ed was not very confiding in those things. He and I would show up at the races, and he'd say, "Here's the car, go win." It was protested several times, but it was a legal car. We had a lot of fun. I enjoyed Ed Brown and I enjoyed racing for Manhattan quite a bit.

The Bristol had a more sophisticated suspension by a whole lot. In the Healey, you had a solid rear axle, differential, and a lot of unsprung weight. In the Bristol you did not. It had an independent rear and less unsprung weight. And a lot less weight, period. I'm not sure about the horsepower between the two engines.

Another driver who raced a 100-6 in the United States was restaurateur Vincent Sardi, who of course also raced a 100S. Sardi, who called his racing activities a hobby, said he didn't quite remember where the race was held, but his last race was in a 100-6.

I entered my Jaguar coupe in the Grand Turismo class. At that time [1955] I had a new business and I was trying to keep that going. My manager at the time was an automobile buff and I had given him the coupe.

Well, I told him, 'I'm going to run this race because I know I can win that.' But when I went to inspection, they told me I needed three new wheels and four tires. My manager said, 'you can't afford that.'

But I had the 100-6 and I kept that in the race. The race started and I was winning. But they had put disc brakes on some of the cars, but not enough. I felt those cars should not have been running in the production class. There were two guys with disc brake cars in the race. I knew what disc brakes were like because the 100S had them.

One guy, I sucked him into a turn, knowing that he could out-brake me, but I didn't think he knew how deep he could go into the corner. He sort of panicked and hit the brakes and spun out. The sad thing is, he hit a flagman, I think.

So there was only one of those guys left. But then I ran out of brakes and I'm not . . . I've seen Walt Hansgen drive a car and win when he ran out of brakes, but I'm not that good. I had no brakes, so I came out of the race, sold the car, and never raced again. That was the end of my racing career.

All who tested the car or who were involved with the development of the car bewailed its lack of performance but admitted that the six offered considerably smoother running than the four.

The BN4 proved to be a transition vehicle in more ways than simply in the engine compartment. The first 6,045 vehicles were constructed at Longbridge as all previous Austin-Healeys (except, of course, the 100S) had been. However, in late 1957, production of the Austin-Healey was transferred to Abingdon to share factory space with the MGA. A total of 4,241 BN4 100-Sixes were built at Abingdon. When the BN6 was introduced, all 4,150 were built at Abingdon, as were all the 3000-series cars.

Shortly after the move to Abingdon, a new six-port cylinder head was developed for the 100-6 that increased power to 117 hp at 4,750 rpm with 149 lb-ft torque at 3,000 rpm. This head was the result of one developed for three twin-choke Weber carburetors that was installed on the rally cars. These engines developed 150 hp at 5,500 rpm. The Healey engine, however, used two semi-downdraft SU HD6 carburetors and had an 8.5:1 compression ratio. You can recognize a BN6 by the canted carburetors, as opposed to the horizontal carbs of the BN4.

As distributed in the United States, the 100-6 with the 117 hp engine had an oil capacity of 7 qt and a cooling system capacity of 12 qt. The gas tank held 14.5 gal.

Steering was by cam and peg with a 14:1 ratio. The 16.5-in diameter steering wheel had three spokes. Up front the independent suspension used wishbones and coil springs, with lever-type shock absorbers and an antiroll torsion (sway) bar. In the rear were leaf springs, lever-type shock absorbers, and an antisway bar. The disc wheels (wire wheels were optional) wore 5.90x15 tubeless tires.

Options included a radio, hardtop, heater, electrically operated overdrive, and wire wheels with "knock-on" hubs.

The new model showed no major changes to the dash or instrument panel.

Dimensionally, the American 100-6 rode on a 92 in wheelbase, was 157.5 in long overall, 49 in tall with the top up (46 in tall with the top down), 60.5 in wide, and had a 5-1/2 in ground clearance.

Competition

The BMC Competitions Department was officially formed in January 1955 and given the authority to enter any BMC cars in competition events. Austin-Healeys were included on this list, though the Healey competition cars were usually prepared at Warwick.

One of the first venues for the Austin-Healey 100-6 was the 1958 Alpine Rally. Five cars were entered–three from the competitions department, one from the Donald Healey Company, and one used by BMC Vice-Chairman George Harriman. Harriman's red and black car was assigned to Nancy Mitchell and Gillian Wilton-Clark. The green Healey went to John Gott and Chris Tooley. One of the three BMC cars was assigned to Pat Moss and Ann Wisdom, who were the top Ladies finishers at tenth overall and fourth in class, despite a slipping clutch. The others went to the teams of Jack Sears/Sam Moore and Bill Shepherd/John Williamson (the latter pair finished seventh overall).

Pat Moss and Ann Wisdom also drove a 100-6 in the Liege-Rome-Liege Rally, finishing fourth overall, first in class, and first among the ladies.

They won the 1958 European Ladies Touring Car Championship and were eighth overall in the Touring Car Championship.

In September, a 100-6 was prepared to attempt to take a group of Class D 2,000–3,000 cc speed records at the Monthlery track in France. The records were held by Citroën. Despite several aborted runs caused by a slipping clutch and broken rear springs, the 100-6 did set a new forty-eight-hour record of 98.73 mph. Later, 15,000-km (97.04 mph) and 10,000-mile (97.13 mph) records were also set, with a top lap speed of 124 mph. Unfortunately, the aimed-for record of 100 mph wasn't reached.

Two-Seater 100-6

Early in 1958, a two-seater version of the 100-6 was offered. Designated as BN6, it received greater approval from enthusiasts who weren't particularly enthused about four-seat (or two-plus-two) sports cars. The unproduced BN5, like the BN3 before it, was a one-off prototype. According

Retaining the oval grille of the 100S, the 100-6 used horizontal bars. The scoop on the hood allows extra air to the engine.

Vincent Sardi racing his 100-6 at Lime Rock Park in Connecticut. Sardi ended his amateur career behind the wheel of a 100-6.

to Graham Robson, the BN5 was designed to be a base model, or entry-level Austin-Healey 100-6, with a single SU carburetor, disc wheels, and no optional overdrive. However, performance of this "loss leader" was considerably inferior to even the standard BN4, and further production or development was never examined. Robson says the one car, with chassis number BN525927 (indicating it was built at Longbridge), was constructed in 1957 and later modified as a Mille Miglia practice car and sold.

Jensen received greater responsibilities after the move to Abingdon. One writer said Jensen ended up doing everything but fitting the engines and gearboxes to the Healey models.

British Motor Corporation advertised the 100-6 as "The Sports-Car of Sportsmen." Ad copy continued, "By land or sea–he prefers his action with dramatic flavor. That's why the Austin-Healey 100-6 is his car. For here is a pulse-quickening blend of superb engineering and sophisticated styling that satisfies his demands. If you are such a man–you owe yourself a test drive." The Healey was "Built to run 'til the road wears out."

In the summer of 1959, BMC introduced a new 2.9-ltr six-cylinder engine. Austin-Healey was the first car to use this engine. When it was installed in the 100-6, the new car became the Austin-Healey 3000.

Free of the additional marker lights and reflectors carried by the later 3000S, the 100-6 is clean and smooth from front to rear.

Chapter 5

3000 Mark I

Once again, Donald Healey was faced with an engine that was reaching the end of its useful life. In this case the engine was the 2.6-ltr BMC "C" engine that had powered the 100-6. The Austin-Healey 100 had first received the BMC six-cylinder engine in 1956, and a year later the needed extra power was provided with the introduction of a six-port engine. Still the performance wasn't up to the standards of the original four-cylinder 100. Fortunately, BMC had a larger, better performing engine in its parts bin to install in the Healey.

Americans were buying 63 percent of all 100-6 production, and 93 percent of production was exported. With his many trips across the Atlantic, Donald Healey had become aware of Americans' biggest complaint against the car: its poor top-end performance. One way to ameliorate this problem was the installation of a larger engine.

The Hambro Automotive Corporation in New York, importers of BMC cars, called Donald Healey "the Merlin of English motordom" for his "ability to wrest eye-popping performance from vehicles built from production passenger car components."

Work on the new engine was begun at Morris Engines in Coventry. The first move was to increase the engine size to 2,856 cc; then to 2,912 cc.

The grille of this early 3000 is identical to that of the previous 100-6. Although the engine was changed from the 2,639 cc unit of the 100 6 to a 2,912 cc unit, little external modification was made to the early cars except for badging. Automobile Quarterly, Roy Query photo

With its new 2,912 cc engine, the Big Healey earned a new designation—3000.

BMC developed a new block which gave larger, siamesed bores. The BN7 had a bore of 83.36 mm, increased from 79.4 mm, and retained the 88.9 mm stroke of the BN4 and BN6. This combination produced 124 bhp at 4,600 rpm and 167 lb-ft of torque at 2,700 rpm, enough to propel the 2,460-lb Austin-Healey 3000 from 0 to 60 mph in 9.8 sec and offer a top speed of 112 mph. Clearly, this was a car that would answer the needs of the American driver with longer stretches to cover than his or her European counterparts.

Also included on the new 3000 were disc brakes. Triumph had begun installing disc brakes on the 1957 TR3, followed by Jaguar and the MGA Twin Cam. BMC wisely chose to add Girling discs to the Austin-Healey 3000 and Lockheed discs to the MGA 1600, which was also built at Abingdon.

Donald and Geoffrey Healey continued to be involved with the development of the cars as they evolved from the 100-6 to the 3000. "We were involved all the way through," Geoffrey said. "We had all the responsibilities for the design. That was one of the things that [Leonard] Lord insisted on, that we retain that. But of course there was a lot of input in the latter years from Syd Enever down at

MG. He was able to get quite a lot done which improved it."

BMC was also involving the Healeys in the development of the Austin-Healey Sprite, which would use the BMC "A" engine. Production of the original "Bugeye" or "Frogeye" Sprite began in 1958, and the car was introduced in May that same year. The Sprite proved to be a hugely popular car, both because of its price and endearing looks.

The Austin-Healey 3000 could be ordered in two-seat (BN7) or two-plus-two (BT7) configurations. The combination worked. Between March 1959 and May 1961, 13,650 Austin-Healey 3000s were produced: 2,825 two-seaters and 10,825 two-plus-two. Of this total, 2,586 two-seaters (92 percent) and 9,956 two-plus-two (92 percent) were exported to the United States. Externally, the only difference between the 3000 and the 100-6 was a small "3000" badge on the newer car's grille.

Donald Healey wrote that there were many features he would have liked included in the 3000, but there simply wasn't enough time to incorporate them. One of these would have been a new gearbox and shifter mechanism; instead these were car-

While many restorers repaint their cars in a two-tone scheme to highlight the style line, the 3000 MkI is still attractive in a single color. Automobile Quarterly, Roy Query photo

Once again, the body badge received a slight modification.

ried over from the 100-6. Healey wrote that the problem was that the shifter was an adaptation of a steering column change. Therefore, the lever was bent backwards in order to bring the shift knob into a convenient position, and some owners complained about excessive pressure required to shift. However, this was still superior to the "interesting" shift pattern of the original 100. A new gearbox casing with a central remote change was under development in 1959.

Donald also complained about the shift knob. With the excessive pressure required to shift, the gear lever knob rubbed skin off the driver's hand. "Nothing beats a large round ball devoid of any markings or sharp edges," Donald wrote.

Healey also built aluminum alloy steering wheels for the 100S and 3000 at Warwick. These were shaped by Cape Engineering of Warwick, with wood laminated on by Coventry Timber Bending. The aluminum-wood sandwich wheel also proved to be safer in accidents because it would deform, not splinter as "some inferior steering wheels" (according to Donald) would.

By Donald's record, the only major complaints about the Austin-Healey 3000 were excessive cockpit heat from the exhaust, lack of ground clearance, and the need for a better hood.

The 3000 was, as the BMC press releases announced, "the most potent car in the short history of this little tiger."

Despite the tough basic character of the Austin-Healey 3000, it is a comfortable touring machine fitted with all the appointments needed to make long, fast trips a pleasure instead of a chore. The combination steel and aluminum body contains room for two vinyl-covered bucket seats and optional occasional seats in the rear. There is a large lockable trunk in the tail, and a parcel shelf under the dashboard runs the width of the car. In addition there are large pockets in each door. Further luxury is provided by a flush fitting ash tray set in the transmission tunnel between the two seats. A tonneau cover that fits over the cockpit is supplied which, by means of a zipper, can be left in place when only the driver is on board. The convertible top and sliding side windows are tight fitting and, with the optional heater, make the 3000 an all-year-round car.

Despite the adulation of the BMC public relations staff, the 3000 did have problems. It was the first Austin-Healey to be fitted with disc brakes, other than the 100S. The Girling discs showed high pad wear, unfortunately, which was one of the problems with the early BN7s. Where the drum brakes would often last for as long as 50,000 miles, the disc brakes were wearing out in an inordinately short period of time. The early cars also had problems with the automatic choke, hood, ground clearance, and excessive heat from the exhaust system.

Austin-Healeys always suffered from low ground clearance. Rallymasters of the era throughout the United States had to certify that their routes contained roads that were "Healey proof," which meant that they didn't have high crowns which might rip off the dangling exhaust system. Normal paved roads usually weren't a problem, but if a road had a high crown or if it was a dirt road with tire grooves, then the exhaust system was in danger.

As Barry Bilbie explained it, "We did a lot of work on the Healey chassis to make it rigid. It had advantages of course because it was rigid, but the disadvantages were that it became a bit heavy and the underslung chassis frame limited the rear suspension, which would cause problems later on, especially with the exhaust system. I think they must have made more money in replacing exhaust systems than they did in selling vehicles. There wasn't a great deal we could do with that."

And with the exhaust system running right under the left passenger's feet (the passenger in right-hand drive cars; the driver in left-hand drive cars), the Austin-Healey could become a very warm car at times. Pat Moss, who rallied Healeys successfully for a number of years, noted that her co-drivers (Ann Wisdom or Pauline Mayman) often traveled with their shoes off and their feet sticking out the window to relieve some of the excess heat.

Roger Menadue said that he felt some of the problems with the 100-6 were overcome with the introduction of the 3000. "The engine was developing more power then, and that overcame some of the problems," Menadue said.

BMC realized that the car [100-6] wasn't selling so well. So they realized that they had to do something and do it mighty quick to keep the sales up.

People knew the problems with the 100-6. People like Tom McCahill used to write in their magazines about it. They said the Six wasn't as fast, even as the four. We had to do something about it mighty quick. We couldn't do much about it without the help of BMC because they stopped making the four and brought out the six.

We found it was a good car for rallies; it was a very good car for rallies. We turned the rallying over to BMC at Abingdon, the MG people. And they developed the car for rallies. And it was very successful. Of course, for absolute racing it was a bit outclassed.

In European rallies, Pat Moss and Ann Wisdom finished second overall in the German Rally of 1959, which was the highest placing ever achieved by a women's team up to that time.

In 1960, the team of Moss and Wisdom was within sight of winning the coveted women's championship again, after eighth-place finishes in the Geneva and Tulip rallies and a second overall in the Alpine. But it was in the 1960 Liége-Rome-Liége Rally where the "girls" made their mark in history.

Not only did Pat and Ann win the rally outright, of the thirteen cars that finished the event, three were Austin-Healeys. It was the first time a British car had won The Marathon and Austin-Healey won the team prize.

Moss and Wisdom were leading going into the final test. But Pat was pooped.

The last test before the easy run back to Spa was on the Granier, and I was so tired by then that I could not hurry any more. I was limp and sleepy and so worn out that 50 kph [about 31 mph] seemed fast. I just could not force myself to go any

The brochure using this photograph identified the 3000 as the "Sports-car of Sportsmen."

quicker, although I was sure we could lose our first place in the rally because of it.

This was supposed to be a speed test, a race against the clock, and I was driving a big, fast car with good road-holding and brakes, yet I was crawling like a snail. I was very cross with myself, yet I could do nothing about it.

It turned out everybody felt the same, and all had pretty well the identical time over the course. So we were still in the lead and held it to the finish. That perked me up, for although I had driven for ninety of the ninety-six hours, the thought of winning the Liége, of all rallies, outright, was the best tonic possible.

Road & Track tested an Austin-Healey 3000 and reported on it in August 1959. Eastern Editor Harvey B. Janes and Eastern Advertising Manager David E. Davis Jr. drove the Healey coast-to-coast in fifty-seven hours. In the test, the *R&T* staffers were able to achieve 0-60 times of 9.8 sec, easily topping the 12.2 sec run in the 100-6. Top speed for the 3000 was 112.5 mph, versus 105 for the 100-6. *Road & Track* gave an estimated list price of $3,395 for the 3000 and calculated fuel consumption at between 17 and 22 mpg. They liked the car, writing that "BMC Rally Team member John Gott wrote in *Safety Fast* magazine that he, too, didn't like the new 3000 as much as his 100-6." In a classic British convoluted sentence, he wrote:

On first taking one over, I, like most of the other team drivers, felt that the new 3-ltr model was by no means an improvement over our rally-proven '100-6s,' which had, after all, in 1958 won a Coupe des Alpes and performed outstandingly in the Liége, where they scored a class win, the Coupes des Dames, and two team prizes. However, with a few hundred kilometers behind me I came to like the bigger car, which was quite a bit faster uphill. In 1958, for instance, the fastest '10-6' on the Stelvio climb did 17 min, 36 sec, but the fastest '3000' cut that down to 16 min, 50 sec in 1959. Downhill, it was a very different story and our first

demand was for better brakes, followed by another for stronger suspension springs.

Eventually, Gott's highly modified ex-works 3000, despite being considerably heavier than the stock 3000, proved to be quicker from 0-60 (10.2 sec versus 11.7 sec) and from 0 to 100 mph (23.9 sec versus 38.3 sec).

Jim Parkinson racing his 3000 at the 1960 Cal Club Re-gionals at the L.A. County Fairgrounds in Pomona. Bob Tronolone photo

Parkinson leading a slew of 1950s sports cars in the same 1960 event. Bob Tronolone photo

Chapter 6

3000 Mark II

BMC and Austin-Healey engineers were always looking for ways to extract more performance from the 3000, and these modifications led to the Mark II and Mark III versions of the 3000. In some cases, too, styling changes helped create new Marks or "B" numbers.

For example, the 3000 Mark II came about when there was a change to a new head using three 1-1/2 in SU HS4 carburetors. This three-carburetor version delivered 132 bhp at 4,750 rpm and 167 lb-ft torque at 3,000 rpm. This was a boost of eight horses over the Mark I but at a cost. Owners of three-carb 1962 3000 Mark IIs, loved these cars but said that even experienced tuners had trouble keeping the carburetors in tune.

In March 1961, 3000 Mark II models received engine type 29E, which had the three-carburetor head. In 1962, however, BMC reverted to using a two-carburetor head on the Mark II, which was designated 29F.

According to Geoff Healey, the change to three carburetors was for competition purposes. "Regulations permitted a change of carburetor size but not the number as fitted to the production model," he wrote.

The 3000 Mark II also introduced a new grille with vertical bars, replacing the wavy horizontal bars that had filled the oval grille since the 100-6. This pattern was repeated in the hood opening.

With the extra pair of jump seats, the spare tire was moved to the trunk, necessitating luggage racks for owners who were interested in travel. Ray Carbone photo

The vertical grille bars of the 3000 Mark II gave the Healey its last major front-end styling change. Ray Carbone photo

Where the hood bulge had three chrome vertical bars connected by one horizontal bar, on the Mark II (and later on the Mark III), an all-vertical pattern was used.

Identification consisted of a new badge. The grille badge, that had served the company well since the introduction of the Healey 100 through the 3000 Mark I, was deleted. In its place was a new badge, installed just over the grille. It had "Austin Healey" (no hyphen) in chrome on a red background and a winged surround. Beneath the Austin-Healey legend was a second line indicating 3000 Mark II.

In November 1961, the Mark II received a new gearbox design with the shifter on the top rather than the side. It was now possible to have a true center gearchanger with a short vertical lever rather than the side shifter with its long shifter arm. Girling disc brakes of 11 in diameter had been introduced on the 3000 "Mark I." About a year after their introduction, dust covers were added. With the 3000 Mark II, a Girling vacuum power assist was added, which became standard on the Mark III.

Dunlop wire wheels were always a preferred option for big Healeys. The original wheels had forty-eight spokes, but from June 1963 to the end of production of the 3000 Mark II convertible, stronger sixty-spoke wheels were used. Whitewall tires were offered as an option on the Mark II and Mark III and, according to Anders Ditlev Clausiger, curator of the British Motor Industry Heritage Trust, possibly on some earlier cars.

The three-carburetor versions were known officially as BN7 and BT7—two-seaters and two-plus-two—although we've already learned about the size of those extra back seats.

BMC produced a total of 5,450 Mark IIs with three carburetors in 1961 and 1962—355 two-seaters and 5,095 two-plus-twos.

The three-carburetor engine was derived from the rally car, one of which carried Pat Moss and Ann Wisdom to the overall win in the 1960 Liége-Rome-Liége Rally, the first ever overall win by a women's team. And while the win was significant, Pat Moss said she never really liked the Healey that much.

Oh bloody, it was hot. It was so hot you could die in it in the summer. So you either took the dust—bear in mind the roads were then dust, gravel and dirt—and you took the sidescreens off and you had air and the dust, or you kept them up and sweated to death. We always had the sidescreens off.

The Healey was also very frightening. If you hit sand or gravel or something like that it was very fearful. You had a tractor engine in front and nothing in back. So it was very front heavy. If you left the road in a Healey you went off front first; whereas with the Mini you went off backside first.

The two-carburetor engine identifies this as a later 3000 Mark II. Austin originally offered the car with three carburetors, but they proved too difficult for mechanics to keep in tune. The two-carburetor version delivered one less horsepower (158) and slightly lower torque, but these minor differences were not revealed in the performance. Ray Carbone photo

In response to demands by owners for more creature comforts, Warwick began to tackle a list of twenty-five changes to the Mark II within a month of the model's introduction. According to Geoff Healey, primary among these changes were modifications to the frame and suspension. "The top of the frame under the axle was cut away and lowered by 1-1/2 in," he wrote. "The top was closed in and the bottom lowered and strengthened at this point. New springs, raising the car by 1 in, were fitted front and rear. The increased rear axle movement enabled lower-rate springs to be used with benefit to ride and handling."

In 1962 and 1963, they built a BJ7 convertible version, which had a two-carburetor head. This engine developed 131 bhp at 4,750 rpm and 158 lb-ft torque at 3,000 rpm. This car also had wind-up windows and a fully folding hood that stowed neatly behind the front seats. With the top stowed, though, seating in those rear seats was reduced even more. In addition, there were folding wing windows in chrome-plated frames. To accommodate the wind-up windows, a chrome plated finisher was fitted to the top of the door, giving it a more horizontal top line. In addition, a wraparound window with a minimum bowing was also introduced, a departure from the past. The original 100 and subsequent models all had flat windshields, even if they no longer folded.

An optional fiberglass hardtop was offered, except for the convertible models. Two different models were offered, for two-seat and four-seat versions of the car. The tops featured a large, curved rear window.

This view shows the rear seating area. While there were two vestigial rear seats that were made available by the longer body, they were of little use to adults or children above the age of about six. They weren't particularly comfortable either, as they had no back rest. Ray Carbone photo

The later version of the 3000 Mark II had a wood-paneled dash and instrument panel, a locking glovebox, and a central shifter in a center console that could accommodate a radio. Ray Carbone photo

Despite one fewer SU carburetor and horsepower, road testers were able to wring 0 to 60 mph times of 10.4 sec out of the Mark II convertible, only 1/10 sec slower than the original 100. Top speed was 117 mph, making the BJ7 the fastest production Healey to date. Typical fuel consumption was around 20 mpg from the 2,562-lb car, as compared to 18 mpg with the three-carb version.

Seat belt mounting points were added to the body structure with the Mark II beginning with chassis number 13751. These mounting points were on the rear wheel arches, on each side of the drive shaft, and on the floor by the sills at the back of the doors.

Later Mark IIs added wind-up windows to a simple door. Wing windows added a measure of ventilation to a cockpit that would often become unbearably hot because of the exhaust pipes running under the driver's feet.

Though brothers only in name, the Bugeye Sprite and the 3000 series share the title for most popular Austin-Healeys. David Gooley photo

Some owners, such as Mike Blatt, installed aftermarket roll bars in their Healeys. Mike Blatt photo

In the Driver's Seat

Mike Blatt bought his Austin-Healey in 1966. Originally it was Healey Blue over white, but it had several colors during the twenty years he owned the car.

"I liked the way it looked," Blatt said. "At that time sports cars were hot. It was cool to have a sports car. I was single then and it helped. . . actually, I met my wife through the Healey. The car turned everybody's heads, including hers. I took her for a ride, and we ended up getting married. Later I got rid of my wife, but I kept the Healey. It was the only thing I kept out of the divorce."

Blatt's BN7 was the three-carburetor version with side curtains. "They went to wind-up windows after about half a year," he said.

The car had a roll bar for safety, but Blatt never competed in races. Although he belonged to three Healey clubs—the Austin-Healey Club of America, the Lehigh Valley Chapter, and the York, Pennsylvania, Touring Club—he used the car primarily for touring.

"There was nothing better than going out in the evening for a ride," Blatt fondly recalled. "The sound of the car was great, and it was something special to be out in the fresh air. I had an Abarth exhaust system on the car, and it made the nicest sound.

"The best thing about the car was its looks. It looked better with the top down. It also looked better than the version with wind-up windows because there was a dip in the doors that you didn't get with the windows.

"The worst thing was the ground clearance; it was about 4-1/2 in. Everywhere you went you had to go over bumps at an angle or risk tearing off the exhaust system. The two exhaust header pipes went into 8 in of flex pipe. The flex pipe kept rusting out every two years. Over the course of time I replaced just about everything in the car. One of the reasons I sold it was because it needed another engine rebuild. Another was because I needed the money to pay for the reception for my wedding to my second wife."

When Blatt sold his car it had about 100,000 miles on the odometer, although for most of the last ten years he owned the car he kept it garaged. During that time he averaged about 200 miles a year. He bought the car for $1,200 and sold it for $9,000 twenty years later.

The 3000 Mark II was the cause of a slight change to the Austin-Healey badge—the addition of "3000 MkII" under the Austin-Healey wings. Mark II was a catch-all *designation, because several changes were made to the model during its existence that would convert it from the underpowered 100-6 to the modern 3000 Mark II.*

Chapter 7

3000 Mark III

With the introduction of the 3000 Mark III, Austin-Healeys reached the ultimate in comfort and convenience, even if they did lose some of their rough-and-tumble sportiness. The Mark III brought polished wood veneer dashes and wind-up windows of the second-generation 3000 Mark II. While these amenities were applauded in the United States, they were decried by purists, those who believe that true sports cars mean wind in your face and as much discomfort as you can bear.

Geoff Healey listed the changes in the Mark III over the Mark II as:

- Increased power.
- Quieter exhaust system with even better heat insulation.
- Greatly improved dash treatment with wood veneered panels.
- An electronic tachometer replacing the mechanical tach.
- Vacuum servo-assisted power steering no longer standard.
- Base price increased by £50 (about $150).

The 3000 Mark III was officially introduced on February 28, 1964, as the Austin-Healey 3000 Sports Convertible Mark III. *Safety Fast* compared the output of the 2,912 cc C-Series engine of the Mark III–150 bhp at 5,250 rpm–with that of the

The BJ8 encountered new federal regulations that resulted in running lights and turn signal indicators in front.

The final iteration of the Mark III saw the addition of front and rear amber turn signal indicators, installed to comply with U.S. Federal regulations. It does give the Mark III a more cluttered appearance than the 100 model of a dozen years earlier, but it also makes the Mark III instantly recognizable.

Mark II–136 bhp at 4,750 rpm. The magazine added, "Early production models have been timed to go from 0–80 mph in 15.5 seconds, yet smoothness and flexibility have not been impaired and fuel consumption figures are, if anything, slightly better than before."

Safety Fast also praised the revised exhaust system, which, it said, "actually contributes to the increase in power, but cuts the level of exhaust noise considerably, making the car much less tiring to travel in on a long journey."

The Autocar described the interior as simply "changed from the functional layout of earlier models to a symmetrical arrangement of wooden panels with a central console merging with the transmission tunnel." Modern drivers will have no problem with this console arrangement, but to a British sports car owner of the early 1960s, this was a radical change.

On the console were the ignition and other switches, with the heater controls above them. A radio, when fitted, would sit at the bottom of the console with the speaker just above it. A remote shifter and ash tray completed the console equipment. Another nice feature was the addition of a fold-down flat cover for the rear seats. This offered a much more agreeable surface on which to place objects you might be carrying than the small rear seats.

According to Geoff Healey, the interior was restyled by Dick Burzi of Austin. Geoff wrote, "The old Healey-designed pressed steel panel which had endured for eleven years was replaced by a central console with instruments and glovebox in veneered wood panels at either side."

Externally, the Mark III BJ8 was essentially identical to the Mark II BN7, especially with regard to the window and door area. Whereas the previous, side-curtained Healeys had a slightly cut-down door, the wind-up-window versions had a chrome strip leveling off the cut-down area to provide a better track for the window.

The biggest change made to create the 3000 Mark III was a 12 percent increase in power with the 2,912 cc engine–up to 148 hp at 5,250 rpm. Finally the Big Healey would have a similar power-to-weight ratio to allow it to compete favorably with the original 100.

This power increase came as a result of two major engine modifications. One was a camshaft with a longer dwell which gave better cylinder filling and made life easier for the tappets. Also, carburetion was improved with the addition of two 2.0 in HD8 SU carburetors replacing the 1.75 in HS6 SU carburetors of the Mark II.

Geoff Healey wrote, however, that changes in oil technology created problems for the Mark III. Specifically, the high film strength of certain oils resulted in the piston rings not bedding in properly, which caused scuffing of the rings and cylinder bores. Also, American manufacturers used an oil of lower film strength for breaking in the engine. This

was generally changed at 500 or 1,000 miles. Healey solved this problem with a new piston ring developed by Hepworth and Grandage, which had a taper on its face and which bedded in quickly. But, "in practice, what we feared would be a major problem, troubled very few owners of the initial cars."

Of interest to Pat Moss and Ann Wisdom, the exhaust system was re-routed. This new exhaust system was designed to meet pending American regulations that were expected to be extended to England as well. Dual exhaust manifolds and flexible pipes fed a pair of mufflers located more outboard of the left-side floor than before. They were actually mounted outside the left channel side member. Dual tail pipes followed the line of the side member and turned across beneath the tail of the car to exit out the right side. This arrangement

The Mark II dash was a full dash, unlike the 100 and 100 Six, with a burled walnut surface, glove box, and provision for a radio.

Some cars are restored to a particular set of rules, some are restored to the owner's taste. This 3000 Mark II was restored to the owner's taste. He chose to have a brass radiator, chromed engine accessories, and chromed wire wheels.

offered slightly more ground clearance, but the Mark III was still an exhaust eater.

Road & Track, in its review of the 3000 Mark III, said the car was "a much more refined car [than the original] although it retains many of the characteristics of the original version, both desirable and undesirable."

Among the desirable changes were the interior ("tarted up," according to *R&T*), the top which could be erected from inside the car, and the windup windows, which offered a degree of weatherproofing even in the winter.

Even though the rear suspension was improved by permitting additional axle movement, *R&T* thought the ride and handling were still "in the classic sports car tradition of the early '50s, before people like Chapman and Cooper had got into the act." Therefore, the Mark III offered a firm ride with a substantial amount of chassis flexing.

But beware, warned the *R&T* reviewers. "In common with rigidly sprung cars of the time, the road-holding of the Healey is quite good on smooth surfaces, but a fast turn on a poor surface may produce surprises, because the rear end has a tendency to jump and skip over bumps."

The Mark III had a revised synchromesh mechanism, which proved to be stronger and quieter than on previous versions of the car.

The Motor pointed out in its review of the Mark III that the production run of the car extended back twelve years and "must be approaching the end of an unusually long and successful line."

It added that "a little of the original Healey 100 still remains: the classic looks, firm ride, only marginal ground clearance, the vintage driving position, and a take-off that few cars can equal regardless of price."

Stage Two

Austin-Healey introduced a Stage Two version of the Mark III after 1,390 cars had been produced, incorporating some changes that could not be included when the model was first shown to the public. These changes were:

- Dropped rear frame.
- Ground clearance increased by 1 in.
- Rear spring rate lowered from 156 to 199 lb per inch. This resulted in increased rear wheel movement which improved the good road holding and ride, according to Geoff.
- Torque reaction arms on the rear axle.

Official press photo of the 3000 Mark III. Donald Healey wrote in his autobiography that, "it was from the great sporting cars of the twenties and thirties, with their singularly static line, by today's standards, that such cars as the Austin-Healey . . . were to develop, with their flowing lines giving the impression of grace and speed, even when they are standing still." Through almost fifteen years of development, the Austin-Healey remained true to the dictum.

This is a particularly attractive red over black BJ8.

Canada. Production ended on December 21, 1967, with chassis number 43025, according to Graham Robson.

MGC and the End of the Big Healeys

In September 1967, BMC introduced a six-cylinder version of the aging MGB, appropriately named the MGC. This car had styling that wasn't all that different from the car that preceded it, except for a pronounced bulge in the hood. The bulge was there to make room for a new engine, a 2,912 cc inline six.

While the dimensions of the engine were identical to those of the Austin-Healey 3000 Mark III, it was, in reality, a new engine. Internally, it had the same dimensions; externally it was smaller and lighter. Peter Browning said of the MGC, in an interview in *Safety Fast,* "It's great. It has all the superb handling and maneuverability of the MGB, combined with the performance of the Healey 3000. What more could you want?"

Healey fans could want more.

Geoff Healey wrote in *Austin-Healey: The Story of the Big Healeys:*

> Two prototypes were planned—the ADO 51 Austin-Healey and ADO 52 MG. The possibility of pure "badge engineering," where one car appears as two models, was not considered. There was tremendous marque loyalty for both Austin-Healey and MG, of which BMC knew and appreciated the value. For the more discerning type of person who bought sports cars, it was essential that the MG and Healey models should be different in appearance and character, whilst sharing the same main body chassis structure.

> The original concept of ADO 51 and 52 as a common MG-Austin-Healey sports car had a good deal of merit, but the final version was a great disappointment to all concerned. After a somewhat confused origin in 1960, it was eventually announced, as the MGC, in 1967. Fifty-six percent of the new six-cylinder engine's weight, with its seven main bearings, was centered on the front wheels. Handling was poor with very strong understeering characteristics. . . It was dropped in 1971, after some 9,000 units had been produced.

> BMC tried very hard to persuade DMH to agree to his name being used on ADO 51. A number of attempts were made to upgrade the car to a form that was acceptable, but all left one with the feeling that the one-piece classic design of the MGB had been butchered to produce a mediocre sports car. . . DMH was undoubtedly right to refuse

- Strengthened front and rear hubs.
- Separate parking and turn signal lamps. This combination gave the Series Two Mark III a totally unique face, which sets it apart from other 3000 models.
- Larger Girling Type-16 disc brakes in place of Type 14.
- Push-button door handles with slam locks.

BMC continued to build the Mark III until 1967, by which time 17,712 BJ8s were built. More than ninety percent were exported, with most of these vehicles going to the United States and

The last change to the Austin-Healey front hood (left) and trunk lid emblems. Dave Gooley photo

to have their name connected with this unsuccessful vehicle.

In an interview shortly before his death on April 29, 1994, Geoff Healey expressed his bitterness about the demise of the big Austin-Healey in 1967, the eventual demise of MG, and near-death of Jaguar.

I think I am very bitter about what [Lord Donald] Stokes did to the Austin-Healey and BMC and Jaguar and MG, you know. All he thought about was Triumph as far as I could see. And that didn't work out well. It was a terrible thing, wasn't it, the TR7? He was a lorry manufacturer—a truck manufacturer. He didn't know one part of a car from the other, really. He couldn't appreciate the points. He was more of a bean counter. No, he was more of a salesman than a bean counter. He wasn't a very good bean counter. He was a good salesman.

There was still some life left in the old chassis. First, BMC began development of a car called variously "XC512," "The Thing," "The Monster," or "Fireball XL5." This featured a chassis with a large central tunnel and extensions that carried suspension units—hydrolastic elements from the Austin 1800. The engine was to be a 4-ltr Rolls-Royce engine used on the Austin Princess R. Geoff Healey called it a monstrosity. It failed, disappearing "quietly in an ooze of silence and security," according to Geoff Healey.

There was another design prepared by Donald Healey Motors, one which almost made it. This idea was to fit the same Rolls-Royce 4-ltr engine into a modified Austin-Healey chassis. Since the engine was almost exactly 6 in wider than the

With the 3000 Mark III, the fuel filler was moved to the rear cowl. Dave Gooley photo

105

In its final form, the 2,912 cc engine in the BJ8 developed 148 hp. Dave Gooley photo

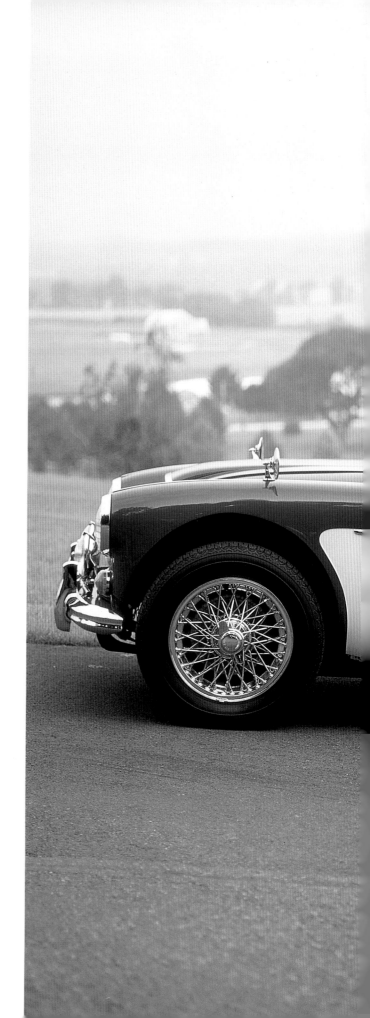

The 3000 Mark III is the ultimate Big Healey. The present owner of this car says the two-tone paint is the result of one of two ideas; the original owner wanted a paint style similar to the 100S, or he was a Penn State fan and simply painted it Penn State blue and white.

"Bluejay 8" looks good even after finishing a pair of endurance rallies in one week. The license plate is a take-off on the model number-BJ8. Owner Jim Cox drove the car in a week-long rally through the Catskill Mountains of New York before heading to Allentown, Pennsylvania, for Encounter 94, the annual meet of the Austin Healey Sports Touring Club.

BMC C-type engine, Geoff wrote that "we cut the whole assembly in half along the center line, and the two halves were accurately aligned at 6 in apart and rigidly fixed. The steel understructure had simple 6-in wide pieces added while the bonnet, scuttle, and boot lid had the pieces welded in and polished smooth."

The Healeys took the car to the powers that be at BMC and the reaction was favorable. Syd Enever of MG was put in charge of the project which was given code number ADO24. Production was to begin in January 1968. But after the first two pilot production vehicles were nearing completion, the project was canceled.

"It could have been built," Geoff said in 1994. "I think Jaguar wasn't in favor of it because it would have clashed, they thought, with their model. It would have been in a similar sector of the market."

So the Big Healey finally died. BMC was concentrating all its efforts on MG and Jaguar on the upper end of the market and on the Austin-Healey Sprite and its badge-engineered twin, the MG Midget, at the lower end. There was no place for the Big Healey to go.

Fortunately, there were places for its creators to go.

Over the years, the Austin-Healey evolved from a brutish basic sports car to a refined grand tourer. These refinements included the addition of windup windows, improvement of the gearchanger mechanism to make it more sophisticated, and the addition of a walnut-cov-ered dash with full instrumentation. The final version of the Big Healey, the BJ8, displays a dash that could easily fit in a sports car of the 1990s from Great Britain, if any remained.

The 3000's front suspension, showing the coil springs, shocks, and antiroll bar, and disc brakes.

The truly dedicated Healey owner will cover the car with an appropriate cover. This one was hand sewn to match–exactly–the car beneath.

In the Driver's Seat

Don Nally bought his present 1967 Austin-Healey 3000 Mk III BJ8 in 1990 because it brought back some good memories.

When I was just out of the army, I had a 1957 Chevrolet convertible, and I traded it in on a 1960 Austin-Healey. Sports cars were very popular at the time. I liked the Healey because it was more powerful than an MG I kept the car four years and sold it when I got married.

I got the bug again after all these years. I always loved the Healey and decided to buy one. I joined the Austin-Healey club in Maryland [Capital Area Austin-Healey Club] to make contacts to find a car. I saw one on the road and asked the owner where I should look. He recommended Bruce Phillips' Healey Surgeons in Takoma Park, Maryland, which is where he bought his car and where I eventually bought mine.

Bruce was restoring the car I bought for his vet, but the vet had to sell it because he needed the money. That's why the restoration isn't complete—the interior still has to be done.

We became involved in the club, and Susan and I go to all the meets. The Sports Touring Club's 1994 Encounter was one of the best meets we've ever been to. The people were nice, and it was really better than the national meets I've been to.

Previous page
BJ8s used more modern Jaeger instruments, the style of which is still used in 1995-era cars.

Top up or down, the BJ8 is a nice-looking automobile. While the earlier Healeys had tops that were difficult to raise and lower, the later models had improved versions that were much easier to work with. The "Convertible" model had a folding soft top that included stiff bars that fitted over the frameless wind-up door windows.

Chapter 8

After the Healeys

After the plug was pulled on the Big Healeys in 1968, the creative minds of the people who made these cars did not dry up. All moved on to other endeavors–some automotive, some creative in other ways. Here is a recounting of just what those people did after the Big Healey.

Barry Bilbie

As with the rest of the Austin-Healey team, Barry Bilbie did not leave the industry when the Austin-Healey ceased production (or rather, when BMC ceased producing Austin-Healeys).

Donald Healey decided to make his own car, tied in with Qvell Kvale, who was from San Francisco. We developed a car for them. I was responsible for the chassis and the understructure of the unibody car. We developed a prototype, and Don and Kvale bought Jensen Motors. Don was the chairman, and I was the chief chassis engineer. I was responsible for the Jensen-Healey, and I took over responsibility for the Interceptor. We did one or two other projects that didn't reach fruition.

Part of Jensen was bought out by Kvale and renamed JSP (Jensen Special Projects). They built special vehicles like the Stowfield off-road vehicle for the army. We built nineteen prototypes before the company ran out of money.

Gerry Coker at Healey's Warwick factory. Gerry Coker photo

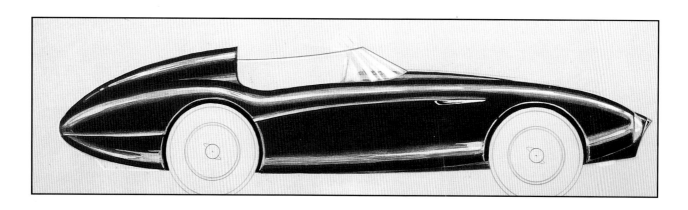

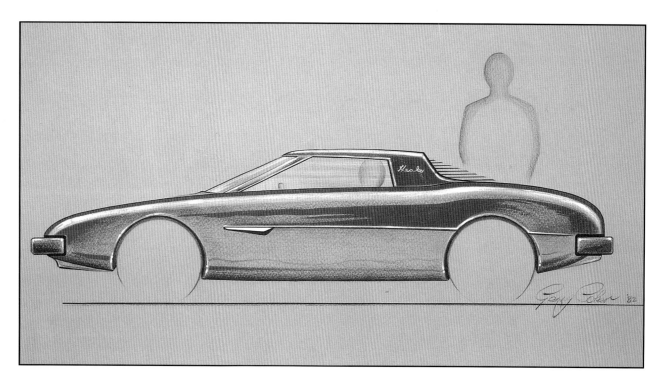

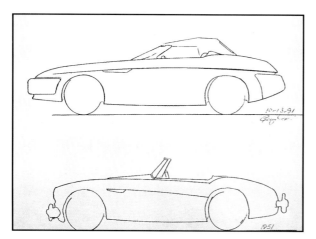

Gerry Coker never stopped "designing" cars, even if none ever came to fruition. Here are some of those designs on a Healey wheelbase.

After the Jensen companies, Bilbie worked for a small company for a few months making locks but said the work "was not very interesting." His next job was with a company that made construction equipment including four-wheel drive tipsters and cement mixers. That lasted for about twelve months.

Bilbie's last assignment was with a company called Hawtal-Whiting, where he was the lead engineer on the Lotus-designed LT5 DOHC engine project for the ZR-1 Chevrolet Corvette. When that project was completed in 1992, Bilbie retired for good.

But, as he often says, he doesn't have much time left anymore, now that he's retired. He's too busy!

Gerry Coker

Gerry Coker left Austin-Healey in 1957 after designing the Frog-Eye Sprite. "I'm not responsible for anything after then," he said recently. He claimed he left England because of the weather, moving first to Detroit. "We thought we'd try the U.S. for twelve months or so; we haven't been back," he said in 1994.

Coker's first job in the States was with Chrysler. "I didn't do any designing," he said. "I was a body engineer." He stayed with Chrysler for five years.

His next move was to Ford, where he finally found a permanent home. Coker's main contribution at Ford was the three-way tailgate on big Ford station wagons that was so popular in the 1960s. "I got a patent on that one," he states proudly.

But Coker was never too far from Donald Healey, even in the United States. Several times Healey asked Coker to pen a design for a car he was thinking of producing. His last design for Healey was a sketch he sent to Don in 1982 for a mid-engine design. The car retains the character of the original Healey and would have made an attractive package if it had been produced.

After retiring from Ford in 1987, Coker and his wife Marion moved to Florida, where they are happily far away from the vagaries of British and Detroit weather. He often travels to Austin-Healey club meets around the country and was a guest at the international meet at Breckenridge, Colorado, and at the 1994 Sports Touring Club Encounter in Allentown, Pennsylvania.

Roger Menadue

After the demise of the Austin-Healey model in the BMC lineup, Roger Menadue moved to Cornwall with Donald where Don had a big house, *Trebah*, which was located on the Cornish coast at the head of a 26-acre valley. Menadue retired to Mawnan Smith and, according to Healey, "was anxious to keep himself active in the sort of work which I envisaged at *Trebah*."

Healey converted one of the many coach houses at Trebah into a workshop for the development of experimental cars. One of these was the first Rolls-Royce-engined prototype; another was the running chassis for the prototype Jensen-Healey.

After the end of the Jensen-Healey project, Menadue went to work for another experimental company which "did one-off things for different people," according to his daughter. One of these one-off projects was a bandage rolling machine.

Roger Menadue seated in a Healey Westland that he had prepared for Tommy Wisdom for the 1947 Alpine Rally. Wisdom won four major trophies in the rally including first place in the 3.0-liter class, class awards for all the speed tests, and first in the concours at the end of the rally. Roger Menadue photo

Eventually Menadue retired, although he remained in close touch with Donald Healey until Healey's death in 1988.

When I contacted Menadue in 1994 for information regarding his Healey years he was most cooperative and a delight to speak with. He supplied many of the photographs of the early years of the Donald Healey Motor Company. However, when I attempted to contact him a few months later for this section of the book, his daughter told me he was off on a month-long camping trip in France to visit friends. He was driving his Ford Escort and had a small stove, a pad, and a few blankets. He would sleep in his car. Roger Menadue was eighty-two in 1994.

Geoff Healey

After BMC discontinued production of the Big Healeys, Geoff Healey retained an interest in the Sprite. "In many years of working with Morris and Austin, and later with BMC, we had developed a great respect for the organization," Geoff Healey wrote. "To us, the Leyland side did not compare with BMC, and we considered their products to be deficient in engineering. Prior to the merger, we firmly stayed in the BMC camp and rejected any possibility of a change of allegiance. After the merger, we were gradually eased out of the picture."

Geoff Healey and Donald in a Nash-Healey before the start of the 1952 Mille Miglia.

In 1967, Geoff engineered the Healey 3000 replacement with the Rolls-Royce engine. In addition, he set up the Healey Automobile Consultants secret workshops in Cornwall to do high security work on vehicles. He was also responsible for the Healey prototype that eventually became the Jensen-Healey. He was named a director of Healey.

Donald and Geoff completed the sale of the company on Geoff's birthday, December 14, 1974. Five years later he joined Rover as a development engineer and ran the Nardo, Italy, tests for Rover. He finally retired in 1989.

Geoff took over the responsibility of being family contact with the Austin-Healey clubs after his father's death. He would travel to the United States several times a year for major club events.

One of these was the Breckenridge, Colorado, International Healey event in 1990. Austin-Healey Club member Bill Bolton of Oregon remembered driving with Geoff after the event and recalled it in *Chatter*, the club magazine: "Geoff and Margot drove my wife Pat's tri-carb 3000 back to Oregon while John and Joy (Healey) drove one of our other tri-carbs. It was a nine-day junket that took us through Jackson Hole, Yellowstone, and central Idaho. During this trip of nine Healeys, Geoff conducted a scientific test of economy on the Healeys and filed a final report on the achievement which started in the number of gallons per 1000 miles."

Geoff was also interested in fishing and boat development and, with Roger Menadue, designed several fishing boats and painted the bottoms with a paint thought to be invisible to fish.

He was continually involved with the development of a company to build the Frogeye, a modern copy of the original Sprite. And he kept the engineering responsibility for the Donald Healey Motor Company until his death in 1994. Running Healey Automobile consultants with Margot as sole directors kept them "very busy and very happy."

Margot Healey said that Geoff was out mowing the lawn on April 29, 1994, when "I took a cup of tea out to him and thought, 'that's an unusual place to be taking a nap.'" Geoff had died from a massive heart attack.

Geoff described what it was like to work with his father in our last interview.

> He never left much to chance. He always thought everything out very carefully. He believed in loads of development and testing. And he believed in what looks right is right. It was a wonderful experience working with him. Every moment. He expected you to work whatever hours were necessary. He'd call you back from holiday and tell you he wanted you to do something. And I think he expected his children to work harder than anyone else. It's a good philosophy. The whole staff believed if he said something it was the right thing.

Donald Healey

Donald Healey never gave up designing cars and inventing new automobiles.

In 1968, the Healey shops in Warwick developed a new Le Mans racer. The 2.0-ltr V-8 Climax-engined Healey SR was a proper race car for its time, with a mid-engine configuration and an aerodynamic body that looked like a combination of a Ford GT40 and a Ferrari Boxer.

The SR used a chassis-platform design, which was similar to that used on the Sprites, rather than the conventional space-frame. The engine, developed with the assistance of Walter Hassan of Coventry-Climax, developed 240 hp and had a top speed of 180 mph. According to Peter Browning in *Healeys and Austin-Healeys*:

> At Le Mans the car was driven by Clive Baker and Andrew Hedges and, although no one expected too much from a lone entry in its first outing, it was disappointing that the car was retired after less than two hours' running with gear selection troubles. However, the car's performance was

certainly competitive for a 2-ltr machine, and this encouraged Healey to enter a slightly lowered and lighter version of the original car for the 1969 Le Mans race, driven by John Harris and Clive Baker. The team suffered very bad luck to have a radiator punctured by a flying stone in the early stages of the race.

In 1972, he and Kjell Qvale, the Norwegian-born supersalesman who originally imported most of the sports cars to the West Coast, worked together to design a new car, then bought Jensen to build it. The car, of course, was the Lotus-engined Jensen-Healey. Unfortunately, the oil crisis of 1976 precipitated the end of Jensen, according to Healey, and the company folded. Healey felt the car they built might have been a worthy successor to the Austin-Healey.

Louise King (actress and wife of Formula 1 racer Peter Collins) remembered that, "after he stopped making the Healey, Donald thought that was the end of him. If he saw a Healey on the road four or five years later, he thought, 'Poor thing, can't get a good car.'"

Healey tried designing boats for a while, and there is an excellent photograph in one of Stirling Moss' books of him and Louise King in a Healey speedboat off the coast of Nassau. And he and Carroll Shelby talked about building a car together when Donald was in his mid-eighties.

But Donald Healey was soon to have a rebirth. "Suddenly he was invited to Australia for the Austin-Healey club out there," Ms. King remembers. This was in 1977. "That started this wonderful old age of Donald's where he traveled and was the guest of Healey clubs. He had a wonderful time. He was a visionary and a well-loved person. His second life was traveling to the clubs."

Healey had unbounded energy. Ms. King tells of when she was appearing in *The Seven Year Itch* in San Francisco. Healey would come visit her and meet her after the show. They'd enjoy the nightlife until the early morning hours when she'd collapse. But Donald was back in his San Francisco office at seven in the morning. "Three hours sleep, four hours sleep, that was enough for him," she said.

Former Saab Director of Public Relations Steve Rossi (now Chevrolet director of product communications) remembers meeting Healey regularly when he traveled to the United States.

I met Donald Healey through my Triumph activity. I had been involved, ever since I was in high school, with Triumphs. I ended up being one

Donald Healey sitting in an experimental Triumph roadster in 1938. Healey worked for Triumph from 1933 until the beginning of World War II, by which time the company had folded and was owned by the Air Ministry. He modified and rallied several standard Triumph models, such as the 1934 Gloria in which he placed third at Monte Carlo. His most successful design, though, was the Dolomite, which was essentially a copy of the Alfa Romeo 2300. Roger Menadue photo

of the early members of what was called the Vintage Triumph Register. It was based in Dearborn, Michigan. I was very involved, and I got on the board of directors and lo and behold, things mushroomed, and I became president of the club. And then I was the [club magazine] editor. Our creed with the magazine was to give people information that they've never found from any other source. My interest in Healey was piqued by his activity—he was chief engineer at Triumph before the war. And he created something called the Triumph Dolomite which was a knock-off of the Alfa. To me [the Dolomite was] the most incredible prewar Triumph that was ever built. So anyway, I was very intrigued by Donald Healey and the Dolomite.

I thought we should have Donald Healey come out and be the guest speaker at the Vintage Triumph convention. I found out that he spent a lot of time in the United States. And he had never been to a Triumph convention. He had never even been asked to a Triumph event. Every one thought oh, Donald Healey/Austin-Healey, he's not our kind. So we asked Donald Healey to come and be our guest of honor at the Vintage Triumph Register National Convention. And he came and that's how I met him the first time.

I have the first letter that he wrote me, framed: "Mr. Rossi: Thank you so much for your kind invitation. I would love to be your guest at the Vintage Triumph Register national convention. Warmest regards, Donald Healey"

He'd call me every time he came to the States. He always stayed at Louise's place in Manhattan. I would get the call, and I would arrange for a Saab press car, because he needed transportation. So I would drop the car off with Louise. He would always drive around in a Saab when he was in the northeast.

It turned out he was a Saab owner. He drove a Saab turbo. He was very excited about a Saab turbo. He was intrigued with Saab, so much so that he had proposed building a Saab-Healey. He wanted to build a sports car—he was eighty-five years old at the time. This must have been mid-1980s—1983, '84.

He became very intrigued with the thought of producing a Saab-Healey. They were doing drawings and everything. I know we had sent him drawings, we had sent him dimensional information and all that for packaging. Nothing ever came of it. At the time he was just too old. He was like an endless tinkerer. And that was probably why he lived so long. His mind was always working. Like I say, the thought of a Saab-Healey was so wonderful.

Louise King remembers that he was staying with her one time after a trip to California to see Carroll Shelby and two good friends—Carolyn Thompson and her sister Marilyn.

I said, "Donald, there's something wrong with you. You're not yourself. I'm going to take you to the doctor."

So I took him to my GP and he recommended a heart specialist. The heart specialist told him, "You've had a heart attack. You must follow a very strict diet and you must not fly yet."

I said, "Donald, don't you remember anything?" He said, "Well, I was getting out of the pool at Marilyn's house in California. And I felt a little funny, but I thought it was just because of her in her bikini."

When he was at the doctor, he told him that he had been in twenty-one airports in the last two months. And the doctor said, "Don't be ridiculous. Nobody can do that." And he must have been eighty-five or eighty-six at the time.

Carroll Shelby called Donald Healey "a very dear friend of mine."

Donald Healey was a very practical automobile man. He knew the specialty business. He knew what people would pay for what. He wasn't one of these pie-in-the-sky guys like you see so often today that think that all they have to do is build something and sell it for a million dollars. He really understood the marketplace and how to coordinate everything with a big company, which I've had to do all my life, too. And that's because we were so close. In fact we were always talking about building another car, right up to his death.

I admired Donald very much, especially his ability to come up with a new, young girl every day—well into his eighties.

Louise King also remembers this facet of the Donald Healey personality. "He was a very friendly man," she said, "and he genuinely liked so many people. He was very gregarious and he loved parties and loved having young gorgeous girls around him."

Part of the legend of Donald Healey was, of course, the cars. But a big part was Healey himself. Steve Rossi defined the man in down-to-earth terms.

I think that he was basically a very, very sincere guy. Here was a guy who was, in a sense, one of the kings of the postwar sports car. He could have been up in the stratosphere. And the guy was at home with anybody and everybody. Yet he'd give from whoever to the Pope the same attention. He was a very sincere person. As old as he was, he had abundant enthusiasm. He'd sign autographs all night long. He'd talk about cars all night long. He could have been a lot different. He could have said, "Oh, get out of here. I'm too important." Not in the slightest.

I have found that there are certain people in this world who really stand out. I found out that one of the reasons they really stand out among the crowd is that they are very sincere and they're willing to give the time of day to anybody. Everybody is an equal. They treat everybody on equal terms. Eric Carlsson is another perfect example. Even a guy like a Heinz Prector—the founder of ASC. He has his own Lear jet. He'll meet you and invite you along on his jet to the next auto show. He's very friendly, very sincere.

Donald Healey was in that same category. To Donald Healey everybody was an equal, no matter where you stood, no matter what your station was in life.

Appendix 1

Specifications

Model	100	100
Designation	BN1	BN2
Production dates	1953-55	1955-56
Number produced	10688	3924
Imported to U.S.		
Engine - Cylinders	4	4
Capacity	2660 cc	2660 cc
Compression ratio	7.5:1	7.5:1
Horsepower	90@4000 rpm	90@4000 rpm
Torque	150@2000 rpm	150@2000 rpm
Carburetors	2xSU H4	2xSU H4
Fuel tank capacity	12 gal	12 gal
Gearbox	3-speed, O/D on 2&3	4-speed, O/D on 4
Rear axle	Spiral Bevel	Hypoid
Steering	Cam & peg	Cam & peg
Wheels and tires	Wire/5.90x15	Wire/5.90x15
Wheelbase	90.0 in	90.0 in
Overall length	151.0 in	151.0 in
Track, front/rear	49.0/50.75 in	49.0/50.75 in
Overall height	49.5 in	49.5 in
Ground clearance	5.5 in	5.5 in
Curb weight	2,148 lb	2,168 lb
Performance: 0-60	10.3 sec	10.3 sec
0-100	N/A	N/A
1/4-mile	17.7 sec	N/A
Top speed	102 mph	103 mph
Price (U.S.)	$2,985	$2,985

Model	100S	100M	100-Six
Designation			
Production dates	Feb. 1955-Jul. 1955	1955-56	Aug. 1956-Mar. 1959
Number produced	55	1159	6025
Imported to U.S.			
Engine - Cylinders	4	4	6
Capacity	2660 cc	2660 cc	2639 cc
Compression ratio	8.3:1	8.1:1	8.25:1
Horsepower	132@4700 rpm	110@4500 rpm	102@4600 rpm
Torque	168@2500 rpm	144@2000 rpm	142@2400 rpm
Carburetors	2xSU H6	2xSU H6	2xSU H4
Fuel tank capacity	20 gal	12 gal	12 gal
Gearbox	4-speed	4-speed,O/D on 2&3	4-speed, O/D on 4
Rear axle	Spiral Bevel	Spiral Bevel or Hypoid	Hypoid
Steering	Cam & peg	Cam & peg	Cam & peg
Wheels and Tires	Wire/5.50x15	Wire/5.90x15	Disc or wire/5.90x15
Wheelbase	90.0 in	90.0 in	92.0 in
Overall length	148.0 in	151.0 in	157.5 in
Track, front/rear	49.6/50.75 in	49.0/50.75 in	48.75/50.0 in
Overall height	42.0 in	49.5 in	49.0 in
Ground clearance	5.5 in	5.5 in	5.5 in
Curb weight	1.960 lb	2,170 lb	2,334 lb
Performance: 0-60	9.8 sec	9.6 sec	12.9 sec
0-100	24.4 sec	N/A	N/A
1/4-mile	16.8 sec	18.8 sec	18.2 sec
Top speed	125 mph	109 mph	105 mph
Price (U.S.)	$4,995	$3,095	$3,195

	100-Six	3000 Mk I	3000 Mk II
Model	100-Six	3000 Mk I	3000 Mk II
Designation	BN4/BN6	BN7/BT7	BN7
Production dates	Aug.1956-Mar.1959	1959-61	1961-62
Number produced	4,214/4,150	2,825/10,825	355
Imported to U.S.			
Engine - Cylinders	6	6	6
Capacity	2639cc	2912cc	29112cc
Compression ratio	8.7:1	9.0:1	9.0:1
Horsepower	117@4750 rpm	124@4600 rpm	132@4750 rpm
Torque	150@3000 rpm	162@2700 rpm	162@2700 rpm
Carburetors	2xSU HD6	2xSU HD6	3xSU HS4
Fuel tank capacity	12 gal	12 gal	12 gal
Gearbox	4-speed, O/D on 4	4-speed, O/D 3&4	4-speed, O/D 3&4
Rear axle	Hypoid	Hypoid	Hypoid
Steering	Cam & peg	Cam & peg	Cam & peg
Wheels and Tires	Disc or wire/5.90x15	Disc or wire/5.90x15	Disc or wire/5.90x15
Wheelbase	92.0 in	91.75 in	91.75 in
Overall length	157.5 in	157.5 in	157.5 in
Track, front/rear	48.75/50.0 in	48.75/50.0 in	48.75/50.0 in
Overall height	40.0 in	50.75 in	50.75 in
Ground clearance	5.5 in	4.625 in	4.625 in
Curb weight	2,354 lb	2,358 lb	2,375/2,460 lb
Performance: 0-60	11.2 sec	11.4 sec	10.9 sec
0-100	37.7 sec	32.8 sec	36.4 sec
1/4-mile	18.1 sec	17.9 sec	18.3 sec
Top speed	111 mph	114 mph	113 mph
Price (U.S.)	$3,395(1958 DeLuxe)	$3,535	$3,371

	3000 Mk II	3000 Mk II	3000 MK III
Model	3000 Mk II	3000 Mk II	3000 MK III
Designation	BT7	BJ7	BJ8
Production dates	1961-62	1962-64	1964-67
Number produced	5,095	6,113	17,703 (17,712)
Imported to U.S.			
Engine–Cylinders	6	6	6
Capacity	2912 cc	2912 cc	2912 cc
Compression ratio	9.0:1	9.0:1	9.0:1
Horsepower	132@4750 rpm	131@44750 rpm	148@5200 rpm
Torque	162@2700 rpm	165@3000 rpm	165@3000 rpm
Carburetors	3xSU HS4	2xSU HS6	2xSU HD8
Fuel tank capacity	12 gal	12 gal	12 gal
Gearbox	4-speed, O/D 3&4	4-speed, O/D 3&4	4-speed, O/D 2,3,4
Rear axle	Hypoid	Hypoid	Hypoid
Steering	Cam & peg	Cam & peg	Cam & peg
Wheels and tires	Disc or wire/5.90x15	Disc or wire/5.90x15	Disc or wire/5.90x15
Wheelbase	91.75 in	91.75 in	91.75 in
Overall length	157.5 in	157.5 in	157.5 in
Track, front/rear	48.75/50.0 in	49.0/50.75 in	48.75/50.0 in
Overall height	50.75 in	50.75 in	50.75 in
Ground clearance	4.625 in	4.625 in	4.625 in
Curb weight	2,375/2,460 lbs	2,375 lb	2,390/2,650 lb
Performance: 0-60	10.9 sec	10.3 sec	9.8 sec
0-100	36.4 sec	29.8 sec	24.7 sec
1/4-mile	18.33 sec	17.4 sec	17.0 sec
Top speed	113 mph	116 mph	122 mph
Price (U.S.)	$3,120-3,438	$3,231-3,535	$3,565

Clubs

The most active and far-reaching of the Austin-Healey clubs in the United States is the Austin-Healey Club of America. Based in Illinois, the AHCA publishes an excellent monthly magazine, *Chatter*, which disseminates information about club happenings, events, personalities, and Austin-Healey history.

Ownership of an Austin-Healey is not a prerequisite for membership. In fact, Don Nally of Maryland joined his local chapter in order to find out where he might be able to buy a Healey.

The major annual event sponsored by the Austin-Healey Club of America is the Conclave, held in the summer, and hosted by a different region every year.

One memorable event sponsored by the Austin-Healey Club of America was held in Breckenridge, Colorado, in 1992. Geoff Healey attended (as he did for many AHCA events through the years), autographed cars, and continued to provide a link with Austin-Healey's past, a link he adopted as his career after the company's demise. It would be the last American event that Geoff would attend.

Most Conclaves will have a concours d'elegance on several levels. For the full-blown serious restorer, there will be a 100-point judging, with penalty points for each deviation from a perfect restoration. For the less seriously minded, there will usually be a fun concours, which is more of a beauty/popularity contest. Here, owners simply show their cars. Attendees at the Conclave can then vote for their favorite cars, with trophies awarded to the top vote-getters.

Conclaves may also include gymkhanas or field trials (depending on insurance regulations), swap meets, model shows, photo and art shows, and seminars on Healey care and restoration. No Healey lover should miss a Conclave.

Membership details regarding the Austin-Healey Club of America are available from Edie Anderson, 603 East Euclid, Arlington Heights, IL 60004.

Subsections of the AHCA are located all across the United States. Here is a listing of some of the sections with contact people. This listing is as complete as possible, but there is always the possibility that one or two have been overlooked.

Alabama
Rodney Martin
85 Rifle Range Rd.
Weumpka, AL 36092

Colorado
Roger Hively (Rocky Mountain)
6745 West Third Place
Lakewood, CO 80226

D.C. (Maryland, Virginia)
Dave Doyle (Capital)
12503 Two Farm Dr.
Silver Spring, MD 20904

Florida
Jim Basque (Orlando)
1633 Dormont Lane
Orlando, FL 32804

Handsome line-up at a West Coast Austin-Healey event. Dave Gooley photo

Don Haugen (Pensacola)
9183 S. Ponderosa
Mobile, AL 36575

Porter Ramsey (St. Johns)
1241 Grove Park Blvd.
Jacksonville, FL 32216

Marion Brantley (Tampa Bay)
2696 66th Terrace S.
St. Petersburg, FL 33712

Georgia
Len Thomas (Central Georgia)
2140 Mountain Lane
Stone Mountain, GA 30087

Illinois
Bill Kowalski (Midwest)
P.O. Box 486
Hinsdale, IL 60521

Ed Kaler (Illini)
5624 S. Washington
Hinsdale, IL 60521

Indiana
Jim Richmond (Indianapolis)
13088 Tarkington Common
Carmel, IN 46033

Jack Summers (Northern Indiana)
204 Westwood Dr.
Michigan City, IN 46360

Iowa
Mark Long (Heartland Healey)
399 Indiandale Rd. SE
Cedar Rapids, IA 52403

Kansas
Gary Hodson (Kansas City)
512 Lake of the Forest
Bonner Springs, KS 66012

Kentucky
Mike Schneider (Bluegrass)
110 N. Rastetter
Louisville, KY 40206

Michigan
Dan Bieniasz (Southeast Michigan)
23800 Evergreen
Southfield, MI 48075

A regular part of most Healey club events is a rally through the countryside, usually unexplored territory for most visiting club members. Dave Gooley photo

Minnesota
Jeff Rossi
3641 DuPont South
Minneapolis, MN 55409

Missouri
John Thousand (Gateway)
9008 Crest Oak
Crestwood, MO 63126

New York
Rick Magro (Niagara Frontier)
210 W. Hazeltine Ave.
Kenmore, NY 14217

New England and Eastern New York
Paul Dunnell (Northeast)
RFD 1, Box 285
Westmoreland, NH 03467

North Carolina
Carl Brown (Carolinas)
7 Pickett Ave.
Spencer, NC 28159

Gary Brierton (Triad)
271 Dalewood Dr. #W
Winston-Salem, NC 27104

Donald Healey signing Dave Venezia's car at Breckenridge, Colorado, in 1985.

New Mexico
Bill Lawrence (Roadrunner)
5521 Sabrosa Dr. NW
Albuquerque, NM 87111-1750

Ohio
Gregg Sipe (Miami Valley)
2058 S. Belleview Dr.
Bellbrook, OH 45305

Nancy Schray (Mid-Ohio)
277 Orchard Lane
Columbus, OH 43214

Don Klein (Ohio Valley)
1370 Karahill Dr.
Cincinnati, OH 45240

Bill Ebersole (Northeast Ohio)
10609 Cedar Rd.
Chesterland, OH 44026

Oklahoma
Wayne McFadden
(Oklahoma Austin-Healey Owners)
6554 S. 100th E. Ave.
Tulsa, OK 74133-1625

Pennsylvania
Bob Gilleland (Three Rivers)
464 E. McMurray Rd.
McMurray, PA 15317

Texas
Mike Johnson (Gulf Coast)
4023 Tennyson
Houston, TX 77005

Jerry Wall (North Texas)
P.O. Box 45332
Dallas, TX 75245

Kate Vogel (South Texas)
8538 Donegal
San Antonio, TX 78250

Utah
Dave Maxwell (Bonneville)
1752 Paulista Way
Sandy, UT 84093

Virginia
Bill Parks (Tidewater)
25 Museum Dr.
Newport News, VA 23601

Washington
Chuck Breckenridge (Cascade)
7015 Olympic View Dr.
Edmonds, WA 98026

Wisconsin
Leroy/Sue Joppa
P.O. Box 131
Laona, WI 54541

Canada
Les Vass (Southern Ontario)
543 Burlington Ave.
Burlington, ON L7S 1R9

Roger Hamel (Quebec)
317 Julie
St. Eustache, QU J7P 3R8

Paul Burnett (Bluewater/Sarnia)
28 Dunkinfield Ct.
Sarnia, ON N7S 3Z3

Austin-Healey Sports Touring Club

This club was formed in 1976 in the Harrisburg, Pennsylvania, area, and, in the ensuing years, has grown from the original five members to over 400. During the growth of the club, it was regionally structured to better serve the localized needs and interests of the mebers. At present, there are chapters in Harrisburg, Philadelphia, and Allentown, Pennsylvania; Wilmington, Delaware; North Jersey; and Long Island, New York. There are also members of the AHSTC who don't live close enough to any region to participate on a regular basis but enjoy the newsletters and occasional events. The regions each have monthly meetings where the members can get together to receive and/or provide technical information, learn of events sponsored by the AHSTC as well as other organizations, locate parts and parts sources, and generally socialize.

The two most important activities of the AHSTC are the newsletter and the annual show, called Encounter. While the newsletter contains information from and for members, Encounter is a chance for all members to get together. Each Encounter features a car show (both popular vote and concours), a rally, photo and model contests, a parts flea market, hospitality room, regalia store, driving events, and awards banquet.

Additional information about the AHSTC and its regions may be obtained from John P. Morrison, 24 Mohr Street, Quakertown, PA 18951. Telephone: (215) 538-3813. Regional information may be obtained from the following:

Harrisburg Region,
Don Schneider (717) 626-8694

Central PA,
Don Hoffer (717) 761-1254

Lehigh Valley Region,
Rick Brodeur (610) 536-6912

Allentown, PA,
Bob Miller (610) 433-1692

Philadelphia Region,
Baird Foster (609) 235-5862

North Jersey Region,
Bob Tebbenhoff (201) 327-4885

Northern New Jersey,
Bob Anderson (908) 852-7966

Many Healey club events are fortunate to have visits from individuals who were important in the development of Healey cars. At Encounter 1994, Gerry Coker was the guest speaker.

Brandywine Region,
Chuck Ott (302) 378-7287

Northern Delaware,
Pete Roberts (215) 458-5412

Long Island Region,
Paul Parfrey (718) 353-8138

New York City area,
Bob Maichin (516) 735-2862

Austin-Healey Club

The California branch of the Austin-Healey Club is known simply as the Austin-Healey Club. Information on this group of clubs may be obtained by writing:

Austin-Healey Club
Box 6197-R
San Jose, CA 95150

In Washington State, there is the Cascade Austin-Healey Club. Information on this organization may be found by writing:

P.O.Box 39
Lynwood, WA 98046

Index